# NEVADA

# BIOGRAPHICAL AND GENEALOGICAL

# SKETCH INDEX

Compiled

by

J. Carlyle Parker

and

Janet G. Parker

Marietta Publishing Company

Turlock, California

1986

Printed in the United States of America

Library of Congress Cataloging-in-Publication Data

Parker, J. Carlyle.
  Nevada biographical and genealogical sketch index.


    1. Nevada--Genealogy--Indexes.  2. Nevada--History,
Local--Indexes.  3. Nevada--Biography--Indexes.
I. Parker, Janet G., 1934-     . II. Title.
Z1309.P37  1986  (F840)   979.3'0016          86-12556

ISBN 0-934153-02-7


OCLC #13642809


$23.95


SAN  693-2002

Marietta Publishing Company
2115 North Denair Avenue
Turlock, CA 95380

(209) 634-9473

To

Max Terrill Greene and Bertha Opal Greene

# CONTENTS

# PREFACE

Biographical sketches are an important secondary source for biographers, genealogists, and historians to consult. Of course, a statewide index to the biographical sketches in city, county, regional, and state histories, and in biographical directories, is a very useful, time-saving research tool. The recent use for genealogical research by the compilers of another statewide biographical index, MICHIGAN BIOGRAPHY INDEX, compiled by Frances Loomis (Detroit: Detroit Public Library, 1946; 4 reels of microfilm; Woodbridge, Conn.: Research Publications, 1973), followed by the consulting of the biographical sketches indexed by it for a particular individual, resulted in the discovery of five earlier generations, including one ancestor who served in the Revolutionary War, and an earlier New England immigrant.

As a result of the successful use of the MICHIGAN BIOGRAPHY INDEX and other such statewide biographical indexes, we decided to prepare the NEVADA BIOGRAPHICAL AND GENEALOGICAL SKETCH INDEX to add to the growing number of these indexes. A list of other biographical statewide indexes is provided in the back of this INDEX on pages 93 through 96.

Many individuals helped us in the preparation of the INDEX. We are grateful to the staff who assisted us in the use of the Washoe County Library, Reno; the Nevada State Library, Carson City; the Noble H. Getchell Library of the University of Nevada-Reno; the Museum-Research Library of the Nevada Historical Society, Reno; the Ormsby Public Library, Carson City; the Genealogical Library of the Church of Jesus Christ of Latter-day Saints, Salt Lake City; the Museum Research Library of the Northeastern Nevada Historical Society, Elko; the Humboldt County Library, Winnemucca; the Bancroft Library of the University of California, Berkeley; and the Genealogical Library of the Idaho State Historical Society Library, Boise. Thanks are offered to Leslee A. Abram and Arthur S. Costa for their excellent service in obtaining books on interlibrary loan that were not available for consultation on earlier visits to several libraries in Nevada, California, Idaho, and Utah. We also wish to thank the several libraries that shared their collections through interlibrary loan, particularly the Nevada State Library, Carson City; Clark County Library District, Las Vegas; and the Noble H. Getchell Library of the University of Nevada-Reno. Thanks is extended to Denise K. Paxton, who assisted with proofreading.

# INTRODUCTION

The NEVADA BIOGRAPHICAL AND GENEALOGICAL SKETCH INDEX is an index to the biographees in biographical and genealogical sketches in eighty-six state, regional, county, and city histories and biographical directories of Nevada published between 1870 and 1985. The names of parents, spouses, children, other relatives, and friends mentioned in biographical and genealogical sketches have not been indexed in this compilation.

The 7,230 index entries include the name of the biographee, a three-letter symbol for the book indexed, the volume number in the case of Scrugham's NEVADA..., and the beginning page of the biographical sketch. Many of the LEGISLATIVE MANUALS have no pagination, but sketches are in alphabetical order; therefore, the word "Alpha" has been used in place of page numbers. Some directories are unpaged and biographical sketches are not in alphabetical order. Page numbers have been provided in parentheses for these unpaged directories in an attempt to assist researchers in their use.

The names indexed were taken from the tables of contents, the lists of biographees, volume indexes, or, when necessary, from the text. Many of the tables of contents provide only the initials of the biographees; and, in most cases, the text was consulted to provide at least one given name. In some cases initials were all that was given in the sketches as well. Names are listed as they were spelled in the histories or directories.

Over one hundred additional Nevada histories and directories were consulted to determine if they contain biographical sketches of genealogical value. The INDEX does not include the biographical sketches of Nevadans listed in biographical directories that are national or international in scope. Such individuals are already indexed in BIO-BASE: A PERIODIC CUMULATIVE MASTER INDEX ON MICROFICHE TO SKETCHES FOUND IN ABOUT 500 CURRENT AND HISTORICAL BIOGRAPHICAL DICTIONARIES, 1984; MASTER CUMULATION (Microfiche, Detroit: Gale Research Co., 1984) or BIOGRAPHY AND GENEALOGY MASTER INDEX (Detroit: Gale Research Co., 1980-  ).

Published single biographies have been excluded from the INDEX. Also not included in the INDEX are the manuscript collections of pioneers in the Noble Museum-Research Library of the Nevada Historical Society, Reno and the H. Getchell Library of the University of Nevada-Reno. Excluded also are the 1964 questionnaires of the family histories of the Nevada Centennial Committee for Early Day Families, which are held by the Museum-Research Library of the Nevada Historical Society, Reno. Additional copies of parts of this excellent collection may be found in other public and research libraries of Nevada.

The Museum-Research Library of the Nevada Historical Society, Reno has an excellent biographical card index that not only indexes some of the books indexed in this volume but includes entries for biographical and historical information found in periodicals and newspapers. Another important reference tool that researchers should consider consulting is AN INDEX TO THE PUBLICATIONS OF THE NEVADA HISTORICAL SOCIETY, 1907-1971 (Reno: Nevada Historical Society, 1977), compiled by Eric Moody.

The books indexed in the NEVADA BIOGRAPHICAL AND GENEALOGICAL SKETCH INDEX are listed in the "Symbols for Books Indexed" following the introduction. They are arranged in alphabetical order by the three-letter symbol used for their identification in the index. The symbols were selected primarily to identify a geographical place or author, title, or subject for statewide histories or directories. Following the index the same titles are listed in alphabetical order by author, or by title, if no author is provided. Most of the bibliographic entries in these lists contain the number of pages in the book, as well as the library book numbers and call numbers, at the end of the citation. This data is included to assist researchers in finding the books. The following is a sample entry to illustrate these book numbers, along with an explanation of the numbers:

Myles, Myrtle Tate. NEVADA'S GOVERNORS FROM TERRITORIAL DAYS TO THE PRESENT, 1861-1971. Sparks, Nev.: Western Printing and Publishing Co., 1972. 310 p. OCLC 668016. LCCN 70-184056. ISBN 0912814011. F840.M94. 979.3/0092.

    OCLC 668016. - The Online Computer Library Center number used by the computers of many libraries.

    LCCN 70-184056. - The Library of Congress Card Number used by the computers of many libraries.

ISBN 0912814011. - International Standard Book
Number used to order books from publishers.

F840.M94. - The Library of Congress
classification or call number used by most college
and university libraries.

979.3/0092. - The Dewey decimal classification
or call number used in most public libraries. Some
libraries use only the 979.3, while others include
0092. The slash mark "/" is a permissive mark
permitting the use of short or extended Dewey
numbers.

Some entries for books that have been reproduced in
microform and/or reprinted contain additional
bibliographic data for more than one publisher.
Occasionally, libraries use the suggested Dewey or
Library of Congress classification call numbers but
change them to fit their special needs. Call numbers
for microfilms available in the Genealogical Library in
Salt Lake City and available through its branch
libraries are included in some bibliographic entries
(e.g. GD 1000194 item 2). Helen S. Carlson's NEVADA
PLACE NAMES: A GEOGRAPHICAL DICTIONARY (Reno: University
of Nevada Press, 1974) and the Rand McNally and Company
COMMERCIAL ATLAS & MARKETING GUIDE, 116th ed. (Chicago:
Rand McNally, 1985) were used to identify the counties
for some of the geographical places not clearly
identified.


A typical INDEX entry is as follows:

    Lockhart, Thomas G.  W07  104


    To locate this sample entry concerning Thomas G.
Lockhart, record the symbol, "W07", and the page number,
"104"; then check the "Symbols for Books Indexed" in the
front of this book, pages xv-xxxiii, to determine the book
represented by W07 (in which the name of interest
appears). Request a photoduplication copy of the
biographical sketch through the interlibrary loan
services of your public library, and provide the
librarian with the author, title, place of publication,
publisher, and date of publication provided in the
"Symbols for Books Indexed," including the OCLC and LCCN
numbers. If any difficulty with a library's
interlibrary loan service prohibits the obtaining of a
photocopy of a desired biographical sketch, ask a

librarian for a copy of the AMERICAN LIBRARY DIRECTORY.
Locate the name and address of the state, county, city
or regional library serving the geographical locale of
interest.  Write to the library directly asking if they
will photocopy the biographical sketch.

Most of the INDEX's 7,230 entries contain useful
genealogical and biographical data.  It is hoped that
through the use of the INDEX, biographers and historians
will find helpful references to data concerning
individuals of interest and that genealogists may find
useful information about their ancestors.  Constructive
criticisms for improvement of the INDEX are welcome.
Please write the compilers at the address on the
copyright page.  Good luck and best wishes for
successful research!

# LIST OF ABBREVIATIONS

Cox Collection   COX LIBRARY: COUNTY, STATE & LOCAL
HISTORIES
>A collection of about 3,000
titles of American local and state
history on 16mm microfilm which is
available in some United States
research libraries and genealogical
collections.

GD   Genealogical Department of the Church of
Jesus Christ of Latter-day Saints, Salt
Lake City, Utah

ISBN   International Standard Book Number
>Used for computer bibliographic
searches and purchasing.

ISSN   International Standard Serial Number
>Used for computer bibliographic
searches and purchasing.

LAC   LIBRARY OF AMERICAN CIVILIZATION
>A collection of about 15,000
titles of American history and
literature on ultra-microfiche,
which is available in many United
States research libraries.

LC   Library of Congress, Washington, D.C.

LCCN   Library of Congress Card Number
>Used for computer
bibliographic searches.

n.p.   No publisher.

OCLC   Online Computer Library Center, Dublin,
Ohio
>This computer system currently
contains 13,000,000 entries to
library materials held in over
6,700 libraries, primarily in the
United States.

s.l.   Without place of publication.

# SYMBOLS FOR BOOKS INDEXED

A82    (Almanac 1982)

NEVADA LEGISLATIVE ALMANAC, 1982. Las Vegas, Nev.:
Ackerman-Rorex Corp., 1982. 279 p. OCLC 9854413. LCCN
82-188376. ISBN 0942112016. JK8531.A63 1982.
328.793/002/02.


A83    (Almanac 1983)

NEVADA LEGISLATIVE ALMANAC, 1983. Las Vegas, Nev.:
Ackerman Information Corp., 1983. 297 p. OCLC 9271007.
ISSN 0942112059. JK8531.N5x. 348.793 N411.


A85    (Almanac 1985)

NEVADA LEGISLATIVE ALMANAC, 1985. Las Vegas, Nev.:
Ackerman Information Corp., 1985. 277 p. ISSN
0942112059. JK8531.N5x. 348.793 N411.


Ame    (American)

American Mothers Committee. MOTHERS OF ACHIEVEMENT IN
AMERICAN HISTORY, 1776-1976: BI-CENTENNIAL PROJECT,
1974-1976. Rutland, Vt.: C.E. Tuttle Co., 1976. 636 p.
OCLC 2369622. LCCN 76-461. ISBN 0804812012.
CT3260.A47 1976. 920.72/0973.
        Only Nevadans have been indexed.


Ang    (Angel)

Angel, Myron, ed. HISTORY OF NEVADA; WITH ILLUSTRATIONS
AND BIOGRAPHICAL SKETCHES OF ITS PROMINENT MEN AND
PIONEERS. Oakland, Calif.: Thompson and West, 1881.
680 p. OCLC 4994580. F841.A5. 979.3.
        Reprint. Berkeley, Calif.: Howell-North, 1958.
OCLC 1865416. LCCN 64-2476.
        Microcard. Louisville, Ky.: Lost Cause Press,
1968. Nineteenth Century American Literature on

Microcards. Series C: The Trans-Mississippi West. 26 microcards. OCLC 1416898.
    Ultra-microfiche. Chicago: Library Resources, Inc., 1970. Microbook Library of American Civilization, LAC 16860. 1 microfiche. OCLC 10955775.
    Microfiche. Louisville, Ky.: Lost Cause Press, 1971. Nineteenth Century American Literature on Microcards. Series C: The Trans-Mississippi West. 26 microfiche. OCLC 4323478.
    Reprint. New York: Arno Press, 1973. OCLC 520660. LCCN 72-9424. ISBN 0405049560.
    Microfilm. Tucson, Ariz.: Americana Unlimited, 1974. Cox Collection: Nevada reel 1:2. 1 reel. GD 1000194 item 2.
    Microfiche. Ann Arbor, Mich.: Xerox University Microfilms, 1975. 11 microfiche. Western Americana 22002. OCLC 5177014.
    Microfilm. New Haven, Conn.: Research Publications, 1975. Western Americana: Frontier History of the Trans-Mississippi West, 1550-1900; reel 11, no. 171. 1 reel. OCLC 3245308.


Arr   (Arrington)

Arrington, Leonard J. THE MORMONS IN NEVADA. Las Vegas, Nev.: Las Vegas Sun, 1979. 67 p. OCLC 8155544. BX8615.N3A77.
    Microfilm. Salt Lake City: Genealogical Society of Utah, 1983. 1 reel. GD 1059488 item 17.
        Originally published in 12 parts by the Las Vegas Sun.


Ban   (Bancroft)

Bancroft, Hubert Howe. HISTORY OF NEVADA, COLORADO, AND WYOMING, 1540-1888. The Works of Hubert Howe Bancroft, Volume XXV. San Francisco: The History Co., 1890. 827 p. OCLC 1722890. LCCN 7-18204//r78. F841.B215 vol. 25. F841.B21.
    Reprint. Santa Barbara, Calif.: W. Hebberd, 1963. OCLC 9592869.
    Reprint. New York: Arno Press, 1967. OCLC 166846. LCCN 67-29422.
    Microfiche. Englewood, Colo.: Microcard Edition, 1968. 9 microfiche. OCLC 7469882.
    Ultra-microfiche. Chicago: Library Resources, Inc., 1970. Microbook Library of American Civilization, LAC 23289. 1 microfiche. OCLC 11024620.

Microfilm. Ann Arbor, Mich.: Xerox University
Microfilms, 1972. American Culture Series, reel 519. 1
reel. OCLC 6748349.
Reprint. HISTORY OF NEVADA, 1540-1888. Reno:
University of Nevada Press, 1981. OCLC 7740971. LCCN
81-13145.
Microfilm. Salt Lake City: Genealogical Society of
Utah, 1985. 1 reel. GD 982474 item 1.
Only the biographees of the brief biographical
sketches of Nevadans found in the footnotes have
been indexed.


Bin   (Binheim)

Binheim, Max, ed. WOMEN OF THE WEST; A SERIES OF
BIOGRAPHICAL SKETCHES OF LIVING EMINENT WOMEN IN THE
ELEVEN WESTERN STATES OF THE UNITED STATES OF AMERICA.
1928 Edition. Compiled and edited by Max Binheim,
Editor-in-chief, Charles A. Elvin, Associate Editor.
Los Angeles: Publishers Press, 1928. 223p. OCLC
2295953. LCCN 28-21005. F595.B59.
Only Nevadans have been indexed.


Bix   (Bixler)

Bixler, W.K. A DOZEN SIERRA SUCCESS STORIES; TWELVE
INDIVIDUALISTS OF OUR TIME: EVA ADAMS, NORMAN BILTZ,
PAUL CLAIBORNE, CLEL GEORGETTA, HARVEY GROSS, RAYMOND
KNISLEY, WAYNE POULSEN, GEORGE PROBASCO, ARCHIE D.
STEVENOT, LESTER D. SUMMERFIELD, HARVEY WEST, JIM A.E.
WILSON. Tahoe Valley, Calif., 1964. 200 p. OCLC
8891407. LCCN 64-16464. F860.B5. 920.07944.


Bru   (Bruner)

Bruner, Firmin. SOME REMEMBERED...SOME FORGOT: LIFE IN
CENTRAL NEVADA MINING CAMPS. Carson City: Nevada State
Park Natural History Association, 1974. 39 p. OCLC
10681996.
The history of Berlin and Union Canyon, Nye
County, eight miles southeast of Ione.

Chr    (Chronology)

CHRONOLOGY AND DOCUMENTARY HANDBOOK OF THE STATE OF
NEVADA.  Chronologies and Documentary Handbooks of the
States, v. 28.  Dodds Ferry, N.Y.: Oceana Publications,
1978.  145 p.  OCLC 4036987.  LCCN 78-16166.  ISBN
0379161532.  F841.5.C46.  979.3/002/02.


Chu    (Churchill)

Herlan, Barbara.  GENERAL HISTORY OF FORT CHURCHILL;
NOTES ON STUDY OF FORT CHURCHILL WITH CORRECTIONS AND
ADDITIONAL INFORMATION FROM FRED I. GREEN.  1 vol.
Carson City: 1964.
        This work has various pagings, the last part,
    thirteen pages, is entitled "Biographies" and is
    the only part indexed.  Fort Churchill is in Lyon
    County.


Cro    (Cronan)

Cronan, John.  NEVADA MEN AND WOMEN OF ACHIEVEMENT.  Las
Vegas: Privately Published, 1966.  Vol. 1.  154 p.


Cur    (Curran)

Curran, Evalin, comp.  HISTORY OF THE ORDER OF THE
EASTERN STAR, STATE OF NEVADA.  s.l.: Order of the
Eastern Star, Grand Chapter of Nevada, 1949.  192 p.


D07    (Dutton 1907)

Dutton, Alfred H., and Lovey, Alan L.  CARTOONS AND
CARICATURES OF MEN WHO MADE GOOD IN NEVADA.  Salt Lake
City: A.H. Dutton and A.L. Lovey, 1907.  (88) p.
        Unpaged, and biographies are not in
    alphabetical order.  Page numbers have been
    provided in parentheses in this index by the
    compilers for ease in locating sketches.

D15    (Dutton 1915)

Dutton, Alfred H.   NOTABLE NEVADANS IN CARICATURE.
1915.   (94) p.
          Unpaged, and biographies are not in
    alphabetical order.   Page numbers have been
    provided in parentheses in this index by the
    compilers for ease in locating sketches.


Dav    (Davis)

Davis, Samuel Post, ed.   THE HISTORY OF NEVADA.   2 vols.
Los Angeles: The Elms Publishing Co., 1913.   OCLC
7990365.   LCCN 15-2825.   F841.D26.
     Reprint.   Las Vegas: Nevada Publications, 1984.
OCLC 11453830.


Doc    (Doctors)

Patterson, Edna B.   SAGEBRUSH DOCTORS.   Springville,
Utah: Printed by Art City Publishing Co., 1972.   196 p.
OCLC 600545.   LCCN 72-93440.   R275.P38.   610/.9793/16.


Elk    (Elko County).

Patterson, Edna B.; Ulph, Louise A.; and Goodwin,
Victor.   NEVADA'S NORTHEAST FRONTIER.   Sparks, Nev.:
Western Printing & Publishing Co., 1969.   702 p.   OCLC
3382780.   F841.P38.
          History of Elko County.


Esm    (Esmeralda County)

Hanson, Herschelle, and Hanson, Genevieve.   THE UNSUNG
HEROES OF ESMERALDA.   Angwin, Calif.: Johnson and
Hanson, Publishers, 1972.   53 p.   OCLC 9839136.
F847.E7H34 1972.
          History of Esmeralda County.

Ete   (Eterovich)

Eterovich, Adam S.  YUGOSLAVS IN NEVADA, 1859-1900:
CROATIANS/DALMATIANS, MONTENEGRINS, HERCEGOVINIANS.  San
Francisco: R and E Research Associates, 1973.  263 p.
OCLC 677066.  LCCN 72-85223.  ISBN 0882471899.
F850.Y7E73.  301.45/19/1820793.


G85   (Grass Valley 1985)

Knudtsen, Molly Flagg.  JOE DEAN AND OTHER PIONEERS.
Reno: College of Agriculture, University of Nevada-Reno,
1985.  11p.
        Joe Dean settled in Crescent Valley, Eureka
    County near the Lander County line and Grass
    Valley.


Geo   (Georgetta)

Georgetta, Clel.  GOLDEN FLEECE IN NEVADA.  Reno:
Venture Publishing Co., 1972.  562 p.  OCLC 507861.
LCCN 70-172916.  SF375.4.N3G46.  338.1/7/63009793.


Geu   (Geuder)

Geuder, Patricia A., ed.  PIONEER WOMEN OF NEVADA.
Carson City: Alpha Chi State of the Delta Gamma Society,
International and the Nevada Division of the American
Association of University Women, 1976.  290 p.


Gil   (Giles)

Giles, Ruth.  RENO LINKAGE.  Reno: Privately Published,
1977.  47 p.
        Reno is in Washoe County.


Goo   (Goodwin)

Goodwin, Charles Carroll.  AS I REMEMBER THEM.  Salt
Lake City: Salt Lake Commercial Club, 1913.  360 p.
OCLC 4636467.  LCCN 13-26259.  F860.G65.

Microfiche. Louisville, Ky.: Lost Cause Press,
1968. Nineteenth Century American Literature and
History. Series C: The Trans-Mississippi West. 5
microfiche. OCLC 1072960.
    Microfiche. Ann Arbor, Mich.: Xerox University
Microfilms, 1975. Western Americana 182021. 4
microfiche. OCLC 5205245.


Gor  (Gorman)

Gorman, Thomas Kiely. SEVENTY-FIVE YEARS OF CATHOLIC
LIFE IN NEVADA: PUBLISHED TO COMMEMMORATE THE DIAMOND
JUBILEE OF THE FOUNDING OF THE CHURCH IN NEVADA, 1860-
1935. Reno: 1935. 131 p. OCLC 6662556. BX1415.N4G6.
282.793.


Gra  (Grass Valley)

Knudtsen, Molly Flagg. HERE IS OUR VALLEY. Helen Marye
Thomas Memorial Series No. 1. Reno: Agricultural
Experiment Station, Max C. Fleischmann College of
Agriculture, University of Nevada, 1975. 120 p. OCLC
1818040. LCCN 74-21486//r82. F847.G7K85. 979.3/33 B.
        Grass Valley is in Lander County near the
    Eureka County line and Crescent Valley.


Hal  (Halleck Country)

Patterson, Edna B. HALLECK COUNTRY, NEVADA: THE STORY
OF THE LAND AND ITS PEOPLE. Reno: University of Nevada,
Reno Press, 1982. 136 p. OCLC 11248612. LCCN 82-
51317. F841.P37x.
        Halleck, Elko County, is between Elko and
    Wells.


Haw  (Hawes)

Hawes, D.C. NEVADA'S CAPITAL AND OFFICIALS. Carson
City: D.C. Hawes (Daily Tribune Print), 1895. (28) p.

Jud   (Judges)

BIOGRAPHY OF DISTRICT COURT JUDGES, BEGINNING 1861.
Reno: 196-   (28) leaves.   OCLC 641852.   LCCN 75-627627.
KF354.N38B5.   347/.793/0234.
        Unpaged, and biographies are not in
alphabetical order.   Page numbers have been
provided in parentheses in this index by the
compilers for ease in locating sketches.


L47   (Legislative)

Nevada.   Legislative Counsel Bureau.   LEGISLATIVE
MANUAL: STATE OF NEVADA; FORTY-THIRD SESSION OF THE
NEVADA LEGISLATURE, 1947.   Carson City: State Printing
Office, 1947.
        Biographies are in alphabetical order.   The
biographies of the Lieutenant Governor, President
of the Senate, and the President Pro Tem of the
Senate precede the alphabetical order of the
Senators.   The biography of the Speaker of the
House precedes the alphabetical order of members
of the Assembly.


L49   (Legislative)

Nevada.   Legislative Counsel Bureau.   LEGISLATIVE
MANUAL: STATE OF NEVADA; FORTY-FOURTH SESSION OF THE
NEVADA LEGISLATURE, 1949.   Carson City: State Printing
Office, 1949.
        See note for L47.


L51   (Legislative)

Nevada.   Legislative Counsel Bureau.   LEGISLATIVE
MANUAL: STATE OF NEVADA; FORTY-FIFTH SESSION OF THE
NEVADA LEGISLATURE, 1951.   Carson City: State Printing
Office, 1951.
        See note for L47.

L53   (Legislative)

Nevada.  Legislative Counsel Bureau.  LEGISLATIVE
MANUAL: STATE OF NEVADA; FORTY-SIXTH SESSION OF THE
NEVADA LEGISLATURE, 1953.  Carson City: State Printing
Office, 1953.


L55   (Legislative)

Nevada.  Legislative Counsel Bureau.  LEGISLATIVE
MANUAL: STATE OF NEVADA; FORTY-SEVENTH SESSION OF THE
NEVADA LEGISLATURE, 1955.  Carson City: State Printing
Office, 1955.  109 p.


L57   (Legislative)

Nevada.  Legislative Counsel Bureau.  LEGISLATIVE
MANUAL: STATE OF NEVADA; FORTY-EIGHTH SESSION OF THE
NEVADA LEGISLATURE, 1957.  Carson City: State Printing
Office, 1957.


L59   (Legislative)

Nevada.  Legislative Counsel Bureau.  LEGISLATIVE
MANUAL: STATE OF NEVADA; FORTY-NINTH SESSION OF THE
NEVADA LEGISLATURE, 1959.  Carson City: State Printing
Office, 1959.
        Biographies are in alphabetical order.  The
    biographies of the Lieutenant Governor, President
    of the Senate, and the President Pro Tem of the
    Senate precede the alphabetical order of the
    Senators.  The biography of the Speaker of the
    House precedes the alphabetical order of members
    of the Assembly.


L60   (Legislative)

Nevada.  Legislative Counsel Bureau.  LEGISLATIVE
MANUAL: STATE OF NEVADA; FIFTIETH SESSION OF THE NEVADA
LEGISLATURE, 1960.  Carson City: State Printing Office,
1960.

L61    (Legislative)

Nevada.  Legislative Counsel Bureau.  LEGISLATIVE
MANUAL: STATE OF NEVADA; FIFTY-FIRST SESSION OF THE
NEVADA LEGISLATURE, 1961.  Carson City: State Printing
Office, 1961.
          See note for L59.


L63    (Legislative)

Nevada.  Legislative Counsel Bureau.  LEGISLATIVE
MANUAL: STATE OF NEVADA; FIFTY-SECOND SESSION OF THE
NEVADA LEGISLATURE, 1963.  Carson City: State Printing
Office, 1963.
          See note for L59.


L73    (Legislative)

Nevada.  Legislative Counsel Bureau.  LEGISLATIVE
MANUAL: STATE OF NEVADA; FIFTY-SEVENTH SESSION OF THE
NEVADA LEGISLATURE, 1973.  Bulletin no. 103.  Carson
City: State Printing Office, 1973.  220 p.  OCLC
1059977.  JK8530.A35.


L75    (Legislative)

Nevada.  Legislative Counsel Bureau.  LEGISLATIVE
MANUAL: STATE OF NEVADA; FIFTY-EIGHTH SESSION OF THE
NEVADA LEGISLATURE, 1975.  Bulletin no. 126.  Carson
City: State Printing Office, 1975.  215 p.


L77    (Legislative)

Nevada.  Legislative Counsel Bureau.  LEGISLATIVE
MANUAL: STATE OF NEVADA; FIFTY-NINTH SESSION OF THE
NEVADA LEGISLATURE, 1977.  Bulletin no. 77-23.  Carson
City: State Printing Office, n.d.  233 p.

L79   (Legislative)

Nevada. Legislative Counsel Bureau. LEGISLATIVE
MANUAL: STATE OF NEVADA; SIXTIETH SESSION OF THE NEVADA
LEGISLATURE, 1979. Bulletin no. 79-21. Carson City:
State Printing Office, 1979. 252 p.


L81   (Legislative)

Nevada. Legislative Counsel Bureau. LEGISLATIVE
MANUAL: STATE OF NEVADA; SIXTY-FIRST SESSION OF THE
NEVADA LEGISLATURE, 1981. Bulletin no. 81-26. Carson
City: State Printing Office, 1981. 268. p.


L83   (Legislative)

Nevada. Legislative Counsel Bureau. LEGISLATIVE
MANUAL: STATE OF NEVADA; SIXTY-SECOND SESSION OF THE
NEVADA LEGISLATURE, 1983. Bulletin no. 83-13. Carson
City: State Printing Office, 1982. 291 p.


L85   (Legislative)

Nevada. Legislative Counsel Bureau. LEGISLATIVE
MANUAL: STATE OF NEVADA; SIXTY-THIRD SESSION OF THE
NEVADA LEGISLATURE, 1985. Bulletin no. 85-12. Carson
City: State Printing Office, 1985. 297 p.


Lab   (Labor)

THE NEVADA STATE LABOR TEMPLE REVIEW: OFFICIAL BUYING
GUIDE OF ORGANIZED LABOR FOR 1914-1915. 112 p.


Lam   (Lamoille Valley)

Patterson, Edna B. THIS LAND WAS OURS; AN IN-DEPTH
STUDY OF A FRONTIER COMMUNITY. Springville, Utah:
Printed by Art City Publishing Co., 1973. 329 p. OCLC
2340007.
          Lamoille Valley is near Halleck, Elko County.

**Lew**  (Lewis)

Lewis, Oscar, ed.  THE LIFE AND TIMES OF THE VIRGINIA
CITY TERRITORIAL ENTERPRISE: BEING REMINISCENCES OF FIVE
DISTINGUISHED COMSTOCK JOURNALISTS.  Ashland, Ore.:
Lewis Osborne, 1971.  53 p.  OCLC 612576.
PN4899.V55L4x.
> Virginia City is in Storey County.


**M15**  (Moore 1915)

Moore, Boyd.  PERSONS IN THE FOREGROUND.  2 vols.  Reno:
n.p., 1915, 1917.
> Unpaged, and biographies are not in
> alphabetical order.  Page numbers have been
> provided in parentheses in this index by the
> compilers for ease in locating sketches.


**M32**  (Moore 1932)

Moore, Boyd.  MEET MR. BY MR. MOORE, IN TWO SKETCHES.
Reno: n.p., 1932.  171 p.


**M50**  (Moore 1950)

Moore, Boyd.  NEVADANS AND NEVADA.  San Francisco: Boyd
Moore, 1950.  216 p.  OCLC 5237055.  LCCN 51-20165.
F840.M6.
> A later printing of this title includes
> supplementary pages 144-A through 144-K, which
> have been indexed in this index.


**M78**  (Mining 1878)

PACIFIC COAST ANNUAL MINING REVIEW AND STOCK LEDGER,
1878-1879: CONTAINING DETAILED OFFICIAL REPORTS OF THE
PRINCIPAL GOLD AND SILVER MINES OF NEVADA, CALIFORNIA,
ARIZONA, UTAH, NEW MEXICO, AND IDAHO; A HISTORY AND
DESCRIPTION OF MINING.AND STOCK DEALING ON THIS COAST
WITH BIOGRAPHICAL SKETCHES OF 100 OF THE PRINCIPAL MEN
ENGAGED THEREIN; AND A SERIES OF FINANCE ARTICLES BY
HENRY S. FITCH.  San Francisco: Francis & Valentine,
1878.  264 p.  OCLC 5897239.  TN1.P2 1878x.

M88   (Mining 1888)

PACIFIC COAST ANNUAL MINING REVIEW AND STOCK LEDGER,
1888. San Francisco: Francis & Valentine; San Francisco
Journal of Commerce, 1888.


Mea   (Meadow Valley)

Panaca Centennial Book Committee.  A CENTURY IN MEADOW
VALLEY, 1864-1964.  Compiled and Edited by Panaca
Centennial Book Committee, Ruth Lee and Sylvia
Wadsworth, Co-chairmen.  Panaca, Nev.: 1966.   278 p.
OCLC 2164421.  LCCN 66-31853.  F849.P3P3.  979.314.
          Panaca is in Meadow Valley, Lincoln County.


Mid   (Midmore)

Midmore, Joe.  FNB: First National Bank of Nevada.
Sparks: Western Printing and Publishing Co., 1975.
177 p.


Moh   (Mohan)

Mohan, Hugh J.  PEN PICTURES OF THE STATE OFFICERS,
LEGISLATORS, PUBLIC OFFICIALS AND NEWSPAPER MEN, AT THE
CAPITOL DURING THE NINTH SESSION NEVADA LEGISLATURE.
Virginia, Nev.: Daily Stage Steam Printing House, 1879.
(72) p.  OCLC 4097423.  F840.M6.
          Unpaged, and biographies are not in
     alphabetical order.  Page numbers have been
     provided in parentheses in this index by the
     compilers for ease in locating sketches.


Mur   (Murbarger)

Murbarger, Nell.  SOVEREIGNS OF THE SAGE; TRUE STORIES
OF PEOPLE AND PLACES IN THE GREAT SAGEBRUSH KINGDOM OF
THE WESTERN UNITED STATES.  Palm Desert, Calif.: Desert
Magazine Press, 1958.   324 p.  OCLC 1806593.  LCCN 58-
2695.  F591.M92 1958.  917.8.
     Another printing.  Tucson, Ariz.: Treasure Chest
Publications, 1958.  OCLC 5278537.  F591.M92 1958b.
          Only Nevadans have been indexed.

My1   (Myles)

Myles, Myrtle Tate.  NEVADA'S GOVERNORS FROM TERRITORIAL
DAYS TO THE PRESENT, 1861-1971.  Sparks, Nev.: Western
Printing and Publishing Co., 1972.  310 p.  OCLC 668016.
LCCN 70-184056.  ISBN 0912814011.  F840.M94.
979.3/00992.


N07   (Nevada 1907)

Nevada State Historical Society.  FIRST BIENNIAL REPORT
OF THE NEVADA HISTORICAL SOCIETY, 1907-1908.  Carson
City: State Printing Office, 1909.  163 p.  OCLC
8565225.  F836.N46 1908.


N09   (Nevada 1909)

Nevada State Historical Society.  SECOND BIENNIAL REPORT
OF THE NEVADA HISTORICAL SOCIETY, 1909-1910.  Carson
City: State Printing Office, 1911.


N10   (Notable 1910)

NOTABLE NEVADANS: SNAP-SHOTS OF SAGEBRUSHERS WHO ARE
DOING THINGS.  Reno: n.p., 1910.  (188) p.
        Unpaged, and biographies are not in
    alphabetical order.  Page numbers have been
    provided in parentheses in this index by the
    compilers for ease in locating sketches.


N11   (Nevada 1911)

Nevada State Historical Society.  THIRD BIENNIAL REPORT
OF THE NEVADA HISTORICAL SOCIETY, 1911-1912.  Carson
City: State Printing Office, 1913.

**N24**   (Nevada 1924)

Nevada. Adjutant-General's Office. NEVADA'S GOLDEN
STARS.   A MEMORIAL VOLUME DESIGNED AS A GIFT FROM THE
STATE OF NEVADA TO THE RELATIVES OF THOSE NEVADA HEROES
WHO DIED IN THE WORLD WAR. Reno: Printed by A. Carlisle
& Co. of Nevada, 1924.   303 p.   OCLC 5373221.   LCCN 24-
27247.   D570.85.N22A5 1924.   412.793 N41ln.
     Microfilm.   Tucson, Ariz.: Americana Unlimited,
1974.   Cox Collection: Nevada reel 2:2.   1 reel.   GD
1000195 item 2.


**N59**   (Nevada 1959)

Nevada. State Library, Carson City. Reader's Service
Division. BRIEF BIOGRAPHICAL INFORMATION ON NEVADA
GOVERNORS.   Carson City: Nevada State Library, 1959.
22 leaves.   OCLC 12256462.   LCCN 59-63284/L.   F840.N4.
          The biographical sketches in this directory
     are not very good for genealogical information,
     but they were included because they have footnotes
     to other national biographical directories that
     contain sketches of Nevada governors.


**N70**   (Nevada 1970)

NEVADA, THE SILVER STATE.   2 vols.   Carson City:
Western States Historical Publishers, 1970.   OCLC
6141207.   F841.N56.


**O'B**   (O'Brien)

O'Brien, John P., ed.   HISTORY OF THE BENCH AND BAR OF
NEVADA.   San Francisco: Bench and Bar Publishing Co.,
1913.   572 p.
          Included in this volume is the BENCH AND BAR
     OF CALIFORNIA.   Only Nevadans have been indexed.


**Per**   (Pershing)

Gardner, Paul K.   NEVADA STORIES: PERSHING COUNTY.   The
Lovelock Review-Miner, 1931-1966.   136 p.

Phi   (Phi Delta Kappa)

Phi Delta Kappa.  WHO'S WHO IN NORTHERN NEVADA
EDUCATION.  A Bicentennial Project of Phi Delta Kappa
'76, Featuring Brief Biographies and Photographs of
Leaders in Education.  Edward H. Howard and E.E.
Loveless, Editors.  Reno: Phi Delta Kappa, 1976.  63 p.


Pow   (Powell)

Powell, John J.  NEVADA: THE LAND OF SILVER.  San
Francisco: Bacon, 1876.  305 p.  OCLC 1625911.
F841.P88.
     Microcard.  Louisville, Ky.: Lost Cause Press,
1969.  Nineteenth Century American Literature on
Microcards.  Series C: The Trans-Mississippi West.  9
microcards.  OCLC 3296720.
     Microfiche.  Louisville, Ky.: Lost Cause Press,
1969.  Nineteenth Century American Literature on
Microcards.  Series C: The Trans-Mississippi West.  9
microfiche.  OCLC 1002657.
     Ultra-microfiche.  Chicago: Library Resources,
Inc., 1970.  Microbook Library of American Civilization,
LAC 16134.  1 microfiche.  OCLC 11525491.


Rei   (Reifschneider)

Reifschneider, Olga.  BIOGRAPHIES OF NEVADA BOTANISTS:
1844-1963.  Reno: University of Nevada Press, 1964.  165
p.  OCLC 1498335.  LCCN 64-25185.  QK26.R4.  925.8.


Ros   (Ross)

Ross, Silas Earl.  BIOGRAPHICAL SKETCHES OF NEVADA GRAND
MASTERS, F.& A.M.; 1865-1970.  Reno: 1970.  99 leaves.

Scr    (Scrugham)

Scrugham, James Graves, ed.  NEVADA; A NARRATIVE OF THE
CONQUEST OF A FRONTIER LAND; COMPRISING THE STORY OF HER
PEOPLE FROM THE DAWN OF HISTORY TO THE PRESENT TIME.   3
vols.  New York: The American Historical Society, 1935.
OCLC 2727175.  LCCN 35-6372.  F841.S35.  979.3.
    Microfilm.  Tucson, Ariz.: Americana Unlimited,
1974.  Cox Collection: Nevada reel 1:3-5.  3 reels.  GD
1000194 items 3-5.


Shu    (Shuck)

Shuck, Oscar Tully, ed.  REPRESENTATIVE AND LEADING MEN
OF THE PACIFIC: BEING ORIGINAL SKETCHES OF THE LIVES AND
CHARACTERS OF THE PRINCIPAL MEN, TO WHICH ARE ADDED
THEIR SPEECHES, ADDRESSES, ORATIONS, EULOGIES, LECTURES
AND POEMS, INCLUDING THE HAPPIEST FORENSIC EFFORTS OF
BAKER, RANDOLPH, MCDOUGALL, T. STARR KING, AND OTHER
POPULAR ORATORS.  San Francisco: Bacon and Co., 1870.
702 p.  OCLC 2678060.  LCCN 6-4477.  F851.S62.
    Microfilm.  New Haven, Conn.: Research
Publications, 1967.  California County and Regional
Histories.  1 reel.  OCLC 6827535.
    Only Nevadans have been indexed.


Sil    (Silen)

Silen, Sol.  LA HISTORIA DE LOS VASCONGADOS EN EL OESTE
DE LOS ESTADOS UNIDOS.  Traducciones por Manuel J. de
Galvan.  New York: Las Novedades, 1917.  Boise: Mountain
States Publishers, 1918.  440 p.  OCLC 8706494.
E184.B15S5.
    Only the Basques of Nevada have been indexed.


Ske    (Sketches)

SKETCHES OF THE INTER-MOUNTAIN STATES: TOGETHER WITH
BIOGRAPHIES OF MANY PROMINENT AND PROGRESSIVE CITIZENS
WHO HAVE HELPED IN THE DEVELOPMENT AND HISTORY-MAKING OF
THIS MARVELOUS REGION: 1847-1909: UTAH, IDAHO, NEVADA.
Salt Lake City, Utah: Salt Lake Tribune, 1909.   376 p.
OCLC 3794451.  LCCN 09-26432.  F826.S62.  917.92.
    Microfilm.  Tucson, Ariz.: Americana Unlimited,
1974.  Cox Collection: Utah reel 3:2.  1 reel.  GD
1000614 item 1.
    Only Nevadans have been indexed.

Suc   (Successful)

The Successful American.  PORTRAITS AND BIOGRAPHIES OF
PROMINENT ENGINEERS, MINERS AND BUSINESS MEN OF
NEVADA....  New York: Writers' Press Association, 1906.
161 p.
        Copy of the The Successful American, vol. 12,
    no. 2.


Tay   (Taylor)

Taylor, Maude Sawin.  FROM MY NEVADA NOTEBOOK.  Sparks,
Nev.: Western Printing and Publishing Co., 1965.  158 p.
OCLC 4491216.  LCCN 78-310475.  F840.T39.  979.3.


W07   (Who's Who 1907)

WHO'S WHO IN NEVADA: BRIEF SKETCHES OF MEN WHO ARE
MAKING HISTORY IN THE SAGEBRUSH STATE.  Published by
Bessie Beatty.  Los Angeles: Home Printing Co., 1907.
276 p.  OCLC 6495690.  LCCN a12-1050.  412.793 B38.
        Microfiche.  Louisville, Ky.: Lost Cause Press,
1968.  Nineteenth Century American Literature on
Microcards.  Series C: The Trans-Mississippi West.  4
microfiche.  OCLC 1015765.
        Microfilm.  Salt Lake City: Genealogical Society of
Utah, 1968.  1 reel.  GD 547580 item 2.
        Microfilm.  Tucson, Ariz.: Americana Unlimited,
1974.  Cox Collection: Nevada reel 1:6.  1 reel.  GD
1000194 item 6.


W31   (Who's Who 1931)

WHO'S WHO IN NEVADA: BIOGRAPHICAL DICTIONARY OF MEN AND
WOMEN WHO ARE BUILDING A STATE.  Vol. 1, 1931-32.  Reno:
Who's Who in Nevada Publishing Co., 1932.  63 p.

W49   (Who's Who 1949)

Walton, Clifford C.  NEVADA TODAY: A PICTORIAL VOLUME OF
THE STATE'S ACTIVITIES.  Portland, Oreg.: Capitol
Publishing Co., 1949.  437 p.  OCLC 9933168.  F841.W3.
Cover Title: CAPITOL'S WHO'S WHO FOR NEVADA, 1949-1950,
COMBINED WITH THE PICTORIAL BOOK - NEVADA TODAY.
          Another printing of this title with the same
     contents has the cover title: CAPITOL'S WHO'S WHO
     IN NEVADA, 1950-1951.
          There is also a 214 page edition of this book,
     with NEVADA TODAY PICTORIAL as a cover title, that
     includes no biographical sketches.


Was   (Washoe Valley)

Ratay, Myra Sauer.  PIONEERS OF THE PONDEROSA: HOW
WASHOE VALLEY RESCUED THE COMSTOCK.  Sparks, Nev.:
Printed by Western Printing and Publishing Co., 1973.
470 p.  OCLC 640965.  LCCN 73-76423.  ISBN 0912814021.
F847.W3R37.  917.93/55/03.
          Washoe Valley is in Washoe County.


Whi   (White River Valley)

WHITE RIVER VALLEY THEN AND NOW, 1898-1980.  Provo,
Utah: Melayne Printing, 1981.  703 p.  OCLC 9389812.
     Microfilm.  Salt Lake City: Genealogical Society of
Utah, 1982.  1 reel.  GD 1035916 item 14.
          The White River Valley is in Nye County south
     of Lund.


Wre   (Wren)

Wren, Thomas.  A HISTORY OF THE STATE OF NEVADA: ITS
RESOURCES AND PEOPLE.  New York: The Lewis Publishing
Co., 1904.  760 p.  OCLC 1541278.  LCCN 18-22486.
F841.W94.  973.W945h.
     Microfiche.  Louisville, Ky.: Lost Cause Press,
1969.  Travels in the West and Southwest.  23
microfiche.  OCLC 11329267.

NEVADA BIOGRAPHICAL AND GENEALOGICAL SKETCH INDEX

| | | | |
|---|---|---|---|
| Abbett, Gertrude H. | W49 | 236 | |
| Abbey, John | Bru | 33 | |
| Abbott, G.D. | Wre | 587 | |
| Abbott, William Eliah | | | |
| | W49 | 236 | |
| Abel, Adele Hammond | N70 | 601 | |
| Abel, John D. "Jack" | Lam | 213 | |
| Abel, John D. "Uncle Jack" | | | |
| | Hal | 71 | |
| Abel, Nellie Van Drielen | | | |
| | N70 | 813 | |
| Abernathy, Lee | Scr | 3:142 | |
| Aboitiz, Angel | Sil | 413 | |
| Abraham, William R. | N70 | 865 | |
| Abrams, William G. | Phi | 25 | |
| Acciari, Joseph | N70 | 885 | |
| Achabal, Anacleto | Sil | 413 | |
| Achabal, Balbino | Sil | 314 | |
| Achabal, Segundo | Sil | 414 | |
| Acrea, Delbert Leonard | | | |
| | W49 | 236 | |
| Acree, Bert | Scr | 3:262 | |
| Acree, Elbert M. (Bert) | | | |
| | W31 | 7; | W49 236 |
| Acree, Thomas S. | Scr | 3:261 | |
| Adair, William M. | N70 | 207 | |
| Adair, Worley | N70 | 249 | |
| Adams, Albert F. | Dav | 1074 | |
| | Scr | 2:154 | |
| Adams, Albert John | W49 | 236 | |
| Adams, Alfred, Jr. | D07 | (23) | |
| Adams, Amy E. | W49 | 237 | |
| Adams, Brewster | W31 | 7 | |
| | W49 | 237 | |
| Adams, Eva | Bix | 11 | |
| Adams, Gary J. | L53 | Alpha | |
| | L55 | 63 | |
| Adams, J.W. | Ban | 321 | |
| Adams, Jewett W. | Chr | 15 | |
| | Geo | 310; | Moh 6 |
| | N59 | 5; | Scr 1:326 |
| | W07 | 40 | |
| Adams, Jewett William | | | |
| | Myl | 31 | |
| Adams, John Quincy | Ang | 382 | |
| Adams, Maxwell | W31 | 7 | |
| Adams, Robert Eugene | W49 | 237 | |
| Adams, Robert Nyle | N70 | 1049 | |
| Adams, Robert Taylor | M50 | 134 | |
| | W49 | 237 | |
| Adams, Wayne B. | W31 | 7 | |
| | W49 | 237 | |
| Adams, William R. (Bill) | | | |
| | W31 | 7 | |
| Adams, William Robert | | | |
| | Ros | 58 | |
| Adcock, Oren K. | Scr | 3:174 | |
| | W49 | 238 | |

| | | | |
|---|---|---|---|
| Aden, John Conrad | N70 | 557 | |
| Agee, Albert Harold | W49 | 238 | |
| Agee, Henry Vance | N70 | 957 | |
| Agee, Horace | Elk | 323 | |
| Agee, Horace A. | Scr | 2:93 | |
| Agee, W. Lester | N70 | 429 | |
| Agrelius, Fred | Lam | 213 | |
| Ahern, John P. | W49 | 238 | |
| Aiazzi, Angelo | N70 | 972 | |
| Aiazzi, George | N70 | 349 | |
| Aiken, Denzel Nelson | N70 | 258 | |
| Ainley, John | Lam | 214 | |
| Aitken, John Hill | N70 | 197 | |
| Aitken, Leonard Charles | | | |
| | N24 | 22 | |
| Albert, Cecil | Lam | 214 | |
| Albiston, Franklin Ray | | | |
| | N70 | 617 | |
| Albisu, Batista | N70 | 610 | |
| Albright, George H. | W49 | 238 | |
| Albright, Jack | W49 | 238 | |
| Albright, Nellie Young | | | |
| | W49 | 238 | |
| Aldaz, J.P. | Sil | 398 | |
| Alemany, Rev. Joseph Sadoc | | | |
| | Gor | 15 | |
| Alexander, A.J. | Chu | 1 | |
| Alexander, Annie Montague | | | |
| | Rei | 151 | |
| Alexander, Isaac A. | Dav | 1082 | |
| Allaback, W. Lloyd | N70 | 291 | |
| Allan, J.E. | Moh | 45 | |
| Allard, Joseph George | | | |
| | W49 | 239 | |
| Allen, Clarence G. | N70 | 1042 | |
| Allen, Doc | G85 | 5 | |
| Allen, George | Wre | 501 | |
| Allen, Harry Samuel | W49 | 239 | |
| Allen, J.W. | Ang | 366 | |
| Allen, James G. | Dav | 1082 | |
| Allen, Jimmy | G85 | 10 | |
| Allen, Lem | Dav | 1082 | |
| Allen, Lem S. | W49 | 239 | |
| Allen, Lemuel | Ang | 366 | |
| | Scr | 3:39; | Wre 317 |
| Allen, Lemuel L. | Scr | 3:41 | |
| Allen, Lemuel S. | Scr | 3:42 | |
| Allen, Lemuel Sparks | Ros | 71 | |
| Allen, Robert A. | Scr | 2:336 | |
| Allen, Steve | G85 | 5 | |
| Allen, Uriah Edward | Moh | 49 | |
| Allen, Valliente B. | M88 | 28 | |
| Allen, Walter S. | W31 | 8 | |
| Allen, William | Lam | 214 | |
| Allen, William C. | Dav | 1083 | |
| Allred, Herbert | Whi | 567 | |
| Allred, Thomas E. | Whi | 603 | |
| Alpers, Ernest J. | N70 | 861 | |

| | | |
|---|---|---|
| Alperson, Wm. | Moh | 71 |
| Alquist, Carl L | Scr | 3:238 |
| Alquist, Lottie | Scr | 3:238 |
| Alt, George | Wre | 438 |
| Altube, Bernard | Elk | 387 |
| Altube, Pedro | Elk | 387 |
| Altuve, Bernardo | Sil | 321 |
| Altuve, Pedro | Sil | 321 |
| Alvy, Richard D. | Was | 102 |
| Alward, Fred S. | Scr | 3:510 |
| Amens, Harold R. | Ros | 61 |
| Ames, Eliot V. | N24 | 23 |
| Ames, Orville | Lam | 215 |
| Ames, William J. | L63 | Alpha |
| Ames, Wiltcie B. | W31 | 8 |
| | M32 | 151 |
| Amestoy, Martin | Sil | 318 |
| Amigo, Fred J. | D15 | (9) |
| Anacabe, Joe | N70 | 409 |
| Andersen, Linford "Digger" | | |
| | N70 | 390 |
| Anderson, A. John | N70 | 941 |
| Anderson, Catherine Smith | | |
| | Per | 18 |
| Anderson, Charles | N70 | 834 |
| Anderson, Charles Lewis | | |
| | Rei | 35 |
| Anderson, Clarence J. | | |
| | N24 | 24 |
| Anderson, Donald M. | N70 | 297 |
| Anderson, Dorothy B. | Scr | 3:187 |
| Anderson, Harold | L49 | Alpha |
| L51 Alpha; W49 | | 24 |
| Anderson, Harold C. | W49 | 239 |
| Anderson, Harold S. | Scr | 3:166 |
| Anderson, Henry | Scr | 3:184 |
| | Wre | 720 |
| Anderson, John | Per | 18 |
| Anderson, John H. | Scr | 2:320 |
| Anderson, Nels | Lam | 215 |
| Anderson, Peter T. | N70 | 642 |
| Anderson, Walter W. | Scr | 3:92 |
| Andrews, George Lash | Moh | 39 |
| Andrews, Harold O. | N70 | 837 |
| Angel, Myron | Ang | 305 |
| Angel, Warren M. | Wre | 487 |
| Anker, Myrtle B. | W49 | 239 |
| Anker, Peter | Dav | 1083 |
| Scr 3:370; Wre | | 630 |
| Ankers, Frank Richard | | |
| | N70 | 952 |
| Annand, George Phillip | | |
| | W31 | 8 |
| Annett, Norman T. | N70 | 1009 |
| Ansolabeher, Jean Maurice | | |
| | Phi | 25 |
| Ansolabehere, John | Gra 92, | 95 |
| Ansolabehere, Mary Jean | | |
| | Gra | 96 |
| Antunovich, A. | Ete | 143 |
| Araberry, Morse, Jr. | A83 | 123 |
| | L85 | xlix |

| | | |
|---|---|---|
| Aramburu, Hermenegildo | | |
| | Sil | 395 |
| Archambeault, Moss | Dav | 1084 |
| Archer, William Andrew | | |
| | Rei | 135 |
| Arcimes, Pete | Lam | 215 |
| Arden, John | N70 | 623 |
| Ardery, Alexander M. | Dav | 1084 |
| Arena, L.P. | Sil | 317 |
| Arentz, Harriet Keep | N70 | 941 |
| Arentz, Samuel S. | Scr | 3:24 |
| | W31 | 8 |
| Arentz, Samuel S., Jr. | | |
| | W49 | 240 |
| Arentz, Samuel Shaw | Scr | 1:511 |
| Arentz, Samuel Shaw (Ulysses) | | |
| | Chr | 15 |
| Arkell, Edwin | Dav | 1084 |
| Armanko, Mitchel | W49 | 240 |
| Armanko, Mitchell | M50 | 138 |
| Armanko, Mitchell L. | Scr | 2:279 |
| | W31 | 9 |
| Armanko, Sam | Ete | 116 |
| M50 116; Scr | | 2:278 |
| Armstrong, Arlo C. | N24 | 26 |
| Armstrong, Mary E. Baldwin | | |
| | N70 | 881 |
| Armstrong, Rev. Robert J. | | |
| | Gor | 31 |
| Arnett, Leonard L. | Scr | 3:29 |
| Arnold, A.E. | Moh | 71 |
| Arnold, Emroy J. | D15 | (7) |
| Arnoldson, Hans Raymond | | |
| | Whi | 582 |
| Arnoldson, Hiram | Whi | 602 |
| Arnoldson, Pharo | Whi | 594 |
| Arnoldus, Margaret Christina | | |
| | Whi | 599 |
| Arobio, Carlo | Per | 75 |
| Arobio, Charlie | N70 | 586 |
| Arrambari, John | Lam | 215 |
| Arrambarri, Juan | Hal | 81 |
| Arrascada, Ignacio | Sil | 322 |
| Arrate, Julian | N70 | 449 |
| Arregui, Frank | N70 | 347 |
| Arregui, Miguel | Sil | 320 |
| Arrild, Andrew | Dav | 1103 |
| Arrizabalaga, Ramon, Jr. | | |
| N70 244; W49 | | 240 |
| Ascargorta, Domingo (Bingo) | | |
| | Bru | 7 |
| Ascargorta, Felicia | Bru | 7 |
| Ascargorta, Felix | Bru | 3 |
| Ascargorta, Firmin | Bru | 8 |
| Ascargorta, Gregoria | Bru | 4 |
| Ascargorta, Josefa Barainca | | |
| | Bru | 3 |
| Ascargorta, Manual | Bru | 3 |
| Ascargorta, Pio | Bru | 3, 8 |
| Ascargorta, Ted | Bru | 4 |
| Ash, Augustus | Scr | 3:123 |
| Ashbaugh, Don | W49 | 240 |

2

| | | | |
|---|---|---|---|
| Ashby, Bryant | Whi | 317 | |
| Ashby, Lillian | Whi | 392 | |
| Ashby, Louisa | Whi | 313 | |
| Asher, John Alfred | Dav | 1097 | |
| Ashley, Delos R. | Scr | 1:271 | |
| Ashley, Delos Rodeyn | Chr | 15 | |
| Ashton, Leonard LaVerne | | | |
| | N70 | 848 | |
| Ashworth, Don W. | A82 | 87 | |
| L79 | xx; L81 | xxii | |
| Ashworth, Earl | Whi | 299 | |
| Ashworth, Keith | A82 | 89 | |
| A83 | 67; L73 | xxv | |
| L75 | xxxv; L77 | xx | |
| L79 | xxi; L81 | xxiii | |
| | L83 | xxvi | |
| Ashworth, Mary Jane | Whi | 253 | |
| Ashworth, Webster (Jim) | | | |
| | Whi | 297 | |
| Aspland, David A. | Dav | 1103 | |
| Aston, M.B. | D15 | (5) | |
| | Dav | 1109 | |
| Atchison, Harry William | | | |
| | N70 | 895 | |
| Atchison, John | Goo | 276 | |
| Atchison, John Barton | | | |
| | Mea | 95 | |
| Atchison, John G. | Wre | 422 | |
| Atkinson, Harry H. | M32 | 87 | |
| | Scr | 3:97 | |
| Atkinson, Harry Hunt | Dav | 1109 | |
| M50 | 92; Ros | 48 | |
| W31 | 9; W49 | 241 | |
| Atkinson, Helen Fuss | N70 | 638 | |
| Aufdermaur, John | N70 | 554 | |
| Austen, Peter Townsend | | | |
| | Suc | 154 | |
| Austin, Charles B. | W49 | 241 | |
| Averill, Mark R. | M15 | (2:7) | |
| Averill, Mark Richards | | | |
| | O'B | 84 | |
| Aylesworth, Arthur J. | | | |
| | N10 | (50) | |
| Aymar, Augustus F. | Ros | 63 | |
| Ayres, Albert D. | Lab | 45 | |
| M32 | 39; Scr | 2:19 | |
| | W31 | 9 | |
| Ayres, Albert Douglas | | | |
| | O'B | 84 | |
| Ayres, Albert Douglass | | | |
| | Dav | 1110 | |
| Azevedo, D.B. | Lam | 216 | |

| | | | |
|---|---|---|---|
| Babbitt, H.S | Scr | 2:445 | |
| Babcock, Jasper | | | |
| Ang | Facing 80; Moh | 12 | |
| Baber, Carroll W. | N70 | 1015 | |
| Bachelor, Arthur Henry | | | |
| | W49 | 241 | |
| Bacigalupi, Frank | L49 | Alpha | |

| | | | |
|---|---|---|---|
| Bacigalupi, Frank J. | W49 | 24 | |
| Backus, Henry Eugene | W49 | 241 | |
| | N70 | 457 | |
| Backus, Lynn F. | W49 | 241 | |
| Bacon, Milton Edward | "Ted" | | |
| | N70 | 896 | |
| Badt, J. Selby | N70 | 629 | |
| Badt, Milton B. | W31 | 9 | |
| | W49 | 242 | |
| Badt, Milton Benjamin | | | |
| | N70 | 830 | |
| Badt, Morris | Wre | 474 | |
| Bailey, David E. | Ros | 12 | |
| Bailey, James C. | L57 | Alpha | |
| L59 | Alpha; L60 | Alpha | |
| L61 | Alpha; L63 | Alpha | |
| Bailey, Joe W. | N70 | 230 | |
| Bailey, John A. | Phi | 26 | |
| Bailey, Mary Rand | N70 | 279 | |
| Bailey, Percy Alford | W49 | 242 | |
| Bailey, Seth T. | W31 | 10 | |
| Bain, Edna L. | N70 | 1051 | |
| Bain, Florence | Per | 134 | |
| Bain, Mary Wright | N70 | 989 | |
| Bair, Maurice | N24 | 28 | |
| Baird, Alexander | Dav | 1110 | |
| Baird, Orval R. | Scr | 3:304 | |
| Baird, Xniea L. | W49 | 242 | |
| Bakeless, Isaac N. | Scr | 2:366 | |
| Baker, B.F. | N10 | (138) | |
| | Wre | 493 | |
| Baker, Benjamin F. | Scr | 3:247 | |
| Baker, Bertram John | W49 | 242 | |
| Baker, C.D. | L47 | Alpha | |
| | L49 | Alpha | |
| Baker, Charles D. | Scr | 3:505 | |
| | W49 | 21 | |
| Baker, Charles Duncan | | | |
| Cro | 4; W49 | 242 | |
| Baker, Charles Henry | Per | 129 | |
| Baker, Cleveland | N10 | (174) | |
| Baker, Cleveland Hall | | | |
| | Dav | 1118 | |
| Baker, E.D. | Goo | 47 | |
| Baker, Eugene Mortimer | | | |
| | Chu | 1 | |
| Baker, Frank | Lam | 216 | |
| Baker, George Washington | | | |
| | Ang | 228 | |
| Baker, Henry | Scr | 3:246 | |
| | Wre | 535 | |
| Baker, John A. | W49 | 243 | |
| Baker, Lloyd H. | Scr | 2:424 | |
| Baker, Maggie | Mur | 184 | |
| Baker, Mary Elizabeth | | | |
| | Whi | 325 | |
| Baker, Phil W. | L61 | Alpha | |
| Baker, Raymond T. | M32 | 51 | |
| | M15 | (1:125) | |
| Baker, Robert William | | | |
| | W49 | 243 | |
| Baker, Stephen | Chu | 1 | |

Baker, Walton Thomas Cur 171
Ros · 77
Baker, William Emmett
W49 243
Balaam, Vera Glaze N70 947
Baldus, Joseph F. Cro 6
Baldwin, Alexander Goo 231
O'B 73
Baldwin, E.J. M78 69
Baldwin, J.E. "Lucky"
Goo 86
Baldwin, Joseph Goo 17
Baldwin, Stanley J. Cro 8
Baldy, W.E. L53 Alpha
Baldy, Warren E. Scr 2:348
Balich, Luka Ete 137
Ball, Carl C. N70 195
Ball, George L. Scr 3:419
Ball, Isaac H. Ang 628
Ballard, G.A. W31 10
Ballard, John J. N70 816
Ballow, John N70 303
Balzar, Fred B. M15 (1:119)
M32 3; N59 16
Scr 1:557; 2:27; W31 10
Balzar, Frederick B. Chr 15
Balzar, Frederick Bennett
Myl 95
Banks, George D. Lam 216
Banner, James J. A82 4
A83 133; A85 135
L73 xxv; L75 xxxv
L77 xxxiii; L79 xli
L81 xliii; L83 xlix
L85 1
Bannister, Alfred C. Dav 1118
Banovich, Nicholas G.
N70 958
Barainca, Andreas Bru 4
Barainca, Bati Bru 3
Barainca, Modesto Bru 29
Barber, Edward Cur 31
Barber, George A. W31 10
Barber, Ted C. N70 562
Barcellos, Manuel F. N70 968
Barclay, W.L. Lam 216
Barengo, Robert R. A82 6
L73 xxvi; L75 xxxvi
L77 xxxiii; L79 xlii
L81 xliv
Barger, Earl U. W49 243
Barigar, Ray Lam 216
Baring, Walter S. Cro 10
M50 74
Baring, Walter Stephan
Chr 15; W49 243
Barker, Don H. Scr 2:283
Barlow, Arthur H. Dav 1119
Barlow, Holman F. "Hank"
N70 310
Barlow, Martha Gruss N70 586
Barnard, William E. M32 167

Barndt, Dick Mur 285
Barndt, Elizabeth S. N70 1034
Barnes, Hillery Lam 216
Barnes, Hillery H. N70 479
Barnes, Millie Whi 606
Barnes, Willis "Bill"
N70 579
Barnes, "Zinc" Goo 307
Barnett, Fielding G. W49 244
Barney, James M. M78 40
Barnum, Bruce L55 63
L57 Alpha
Barnum, Lauren Whi 14, 286
Baroni, Armando Lam 216
Baroni, Eugene Lam 217
Baroni, Julio Lam 217
Baroni, Torelo Lam 217
Barovich, Nikola Ete 22
Barr, A.C. W49 24
Barr, A.C. "Andy" L47 Alpha
L49 Alpha; L51 Alpha
L53 Alpha; L55 63
Barrett, Albert James
Ang 407
Barrett, Charles Harry
Wre 553
Barrett, John S. W49 244
Barrett, John W. Jud (24)
Barrett, Mary Jo Phi 26
Barron, Alexander Franklin
Mea 97
Barry, Norman J. W31 10
M32 19
Bartholomew, Ramond Jackson
W31 11
Bartine, Fred Scr 3:313
Bartine, H.F. Dav 1074
Bartine, Horace F. M15 (1:45)
Bartine, Horace Franklin
Chr 15; O'B 84
Wre 610
Bartlett, Byron, Jr. W49 244
Bartlett, George A. Jud (15)
M15 (1:97); M32 35
N10 (56); O'B 85
Scr 1:434; W07 30
Bartlett, George Arthur
Chr 15
Bartlett, Henry J. W07 250
Bartlett, John G. W49 244
Bartlett, Robert B. W49 244
Bartley, David Preston
W31 11
Barton, Freda Inman N70 551
Barton, George Chester
N70 648
Barton, James F. W49 245
Baskin, Robert T. W49 245
Bass, Joe W49 245
Bassman, Richard W. Dav 1117
Basso, David N70 191
Basta, Sam M. Phi 27

4

Bastein, Eugene          Doc    160  
Bastian, C.O.            L49  Alpha  
                         W49     25  
Bastian, Cyril O.        L51  Alpha  
         L53 Alpha; L55     64  
         L59 Alpha; L60  Alpha  
         L61 Alpha; L63  Alpha  
Bastida, Manuel          Lam    217  
Batchelder, Frank P.     N70    527  
Batchelder, George E.  
                         Scr  3:336  
Bates, Donald B.         W49    245  
Bates, O.G.              D07   (12)  
Bates, Osmond G.         Scr  2:423  
Bates, Osmond George     Dav   1111  
         M50 144-C; W49    245  
Bath, Daryl C.           N70    833  
Bath, Earl               W31     11  
Bath, Ernest H.          W49    245  
Bath, Thomas O.          N70    381  
Batt, F.E.               L49  Alpha  
                         W49     25  
Batterman, C.C.          Moh     66  
Battin, Clarence B.      Scr  3:252  
Battin, Joshua M.        N24     27  
Baumann, Emil            Gra      9  
Baumann, Walter E.       N70   1044  
Baumbach, Chris          Lam    217  
Baumbach, Mel            N70    951  
Bawrley, "Cap"           Bru     28  
Baxter, Ella Victoria  
                         Whi    328  
Baxter, Harold           W07    154  
Baxter, John             N70    316  
Bay, J.L.                L63  Alpha  
Bay, Jack L.             N70   1040  
Bay, Jack W.             L59  Alpha  
                         L60  Alpha  
Bayley, Judith           Cro     12  
Bayley, Warren Vance     Cro     14  
Baylis, Ethel            Whi    588  
Beall, Olin L.           N70    653  
Bean, George Washington  
                         Arr     22  
Bean, James H.           Phi     28  
Bear, Paul W.            N70    486  
Beard, Stephen McGaff  
                         Moh     54  
Beards, Anna             W49    246  
Beasley, Bud L.          Phi     28  
Beatty, Robert Muir      Haw     14  
Beatty, W.H.             Moh      8  
Beaulieu, Cyril          Lam    217  
Beck, Ferdinand          Scr  3:343  
Beck, Henry Hudson       Was    273  
                         Wre    736  
Beck, Henry L.           Dav   1121  
Becker, John J.          Scr  3:115  
Becker, W.S.             Lam    218  
Becker, William L.       Lam    217  
Becker-Jurgen, Leonard  
                         Mur     42  

Beckey, James            Geo    293  
Beckley, Will            N70    210  
                         W49    246  
Bedrosian, Tod           L79  xliii  
Bee, F.A.                Ban    228  
Beebe, Graham H.         Dav   1111  
Beedle, Hadley S.        W49    246  
Beemer, Charles A.       Ros     33  
         Scr 2:132; W49    246  
Beemer, Elwood H.        M32    127  
                         Ros     66  
Beemer, Wm. R.           L47  Alpha  
Beemer, William Russell  
                         W49    246  
Beery, Joseph L.         N70    576  
Behn, William            Lam    218  
Behrmann, Anne           Whi    583  
Behrmann, Cord Henry     Dav   1128  
Behrmann, Heber          Whi    571  
Behrmann, Henry          Whi    571  
Behrmann, Nettie         Whi    571  
Beitia, Fred G.          N70    358  
Beko, William            L53  Alpha  
Belanger, George L.      Scr  3:159  
Belaustegui, Leon        N70    422  
Belding, Ray Jessie      W31     11  
Belew, Ruth S.           W49    247  
Belford, John S.         W31     11  
Belford, John Stuart     Jud   (19)  
         M50 144-A; W49    247  
Belford, Samuel W.       Lab     22  
         O'B  85; Scr 2:373  
Belingheri, Dominick     W49    247  
Belknap, Charles H.      Haw     22  
Belknap, Charles Henry  
         Dav 1128; Wre    380  
Bell, Billie             Bru     17  
Bell, Elmer Jefferson  
                         N24     30  
Bell, Frank              Chr     15  
         N59  7; Myl     43  
         Ros  19; Scr 2:248  
Bell, Frank E.           W49    247  
Bell, Grace Woodward     N70    562  
Bell, Joe                Bru 15, 17  
Bell, Norman             W31     11  
Bell, Rex   Cro  16; L59 Alpha  
         L60 Alpha; L61 Alpha  
         L55  57; L57 Alpha  
                         W49    247  
Bell, Thomas             M78     40  
                         M88     38  
Bell, Thomas Jefferson  
         M15 (2:69); W07     86  
Bell, W.H.               Lam    218  
Bell, Walter             N70    893  
Bellam, Thomas L.        Cur     45  
Belleville, Raymond      N70    586  
Belli, Joe               Bru 15, 17  
Bellinger, Harold        W49    247  
Bellinger, James         Lam    218  
Bellinger, "Lew"         Lam    218

Bellinger, Lewis Carlton
               N70    539
Bellinger, Lewis, Jr.
               Lam    218
Bellinger, Richard "Dick"
               Lam    219
Bellinger, William  Lam    219
Bellinger, William L.
               N70    534
Belmonte, Angelo    Scr 2:343
Bemmer, Elwood H.   M32    127
Benane, Ed         N10  (134)
Bence, Horace H.    Ang    536
Bender, Edwin S.    W49    248
Benedict, John M.   Scr 3:255
Benevent, John     N24     31
Bengoa, Domingo    Sil    412
Bengoa, Francisco   Sil    412
Bengochea, Frank M.  N70    473
               W49    248
Bengochea, Pete Louis
               N70    474
Benham, Guy E.     W49    248
Benkovich, Robert M. L75 xxxvi
Bennett, Blanche Leavitt
               N70    304
Bennett, Darrell    Doc    164
Bennett, Henry Frederick
               W49    248
Bennett, Marion D.   A82      8
       L73 xxvi; L75 xxxvii
       L77 xxxiv; L79  xliv
               L81    xlv
Bennetts, Emma N.   Scr 3:420
Bennioff, Hugo     Lam    219
Benson, Byron Noval  Doc    167
Bentley, Richard    Was    122
Benton, J.M.       Ang    561
Benton, James M.    N10  (124)
Berg, Andrew (Andy)  Lam    219
Berg, Katie Rogers   N70    953
Berg, William H.    N70   1047
Bergevin, Louis W.   A82     10
        A83   217; A85    219
       L75 xxxvii; L77  xxxiv
       L79    xlv; L81   xlvi
       L83      1; L85     li
Bergman, George     Dav  1256
Berk, George       Wre    694
Berk, Henry Leland   N70    192
Berkley, Shelley L.  A83    139
               L83     li
Bernard, Arthur E.   W49    249
Bernard, Victor     N70    992
Bernsen, James      Whi    580
Berrum, Henry W.    L53 Alpha
       L55    64; L57 Alpha
       L59 Alpha; L60 Alpha
       L61 Alpha; L63 Alpha
Berrum, Henry William "Bud"
               N70    897
Berrum, Louis      Wre    674

Bertolino, Pete     N70    920
Bett, John Campbell  N24     32
Betteridge, Wallace H.
               N70    492
Bettles, Gordon W.   N70  1016
Beuhanon, Charles Ellis
               N24     34
Bevard, Douglas C.   N70    448
Bevis, Edward       M32    121
Beyer, Erik        A82     12
        A83   172; A85    174
        L81  xlvi; L83   lii
               L85   lii
Beyer, John Alfred   W49    249
Biale, Albert F.    N70  1028
               W49    249
Biale, J.B.        W31     11
Biale, John B.      Scr  2:91
               W49    249
Bianchini, Joseph   Dav  1126
Bible, Alan        Cro     18
       M50 144-B; W49    249
Bible, Alan Harvey   Chr     15
Bickerstaff, William L73 xxvii
Bicknell, Charles F. Ang    558
               Moh     50
Bidart, Louie      N70    457
Bidleman, George B.  Dav  1126
Bidwell, John      Goo      9
Biegler, Harold     Lam    220
Bieroth, Hugh C.    N70    395
Bigelow, R.R.      Haw     20
Bigelow, Rensselaer H.
             O'B 36, 51
Biggs, W.M. "Windy" Lam    220
Bilbao, Cruz       Lam    220
Bilbao, Dan        N70  1022
Bilbao, David      Lam    220
Bilboa, Cruz       Hal    114
Bilbray, James H.    A82     91
        A83    72; A85     74
        L81   xxiv; L83 xxvii
               L85   xxvi
Bill, Josephine Divingnzzo
               N70    340
Billett, James, Jr.  Lam    220
Billinghurst, Benson Dillon
               Dav  1127
Billings, Irene     Per    135
Billings, J.J.      Lam    220
Billings, William Dwight
               Rei    149
Billings, William E. Dav  1127
               O'B     85
Biltz, Norman      Bix     27
               W49    250
Biltz, Norman H.    W31     12
Biltz, Norman Henry  M50     98
Bilyeu, Byron (Bill) A83    199
      A85   201; L85   liii
Bingham, Dean      W49    250

Bingham, Richard Dean
N70 354
Birdzell, Virgil W. N70 461
Birks, George L. W49 250
Birnie, John Mur 76
Bishop, Harry Mur 206
Bishop, M.M. L63 Alpha
Bisoni, Lester L47 Alpha
L49 Alpha
Bisoni, Lester A. W49 25, 250
Bissett, J. Roger L59 Alpha
L60 Alpha; L61 Alpha
L63 Alpha
Bixby, Frederick L. Scr 2:260
W31 12
Black, Fred D. Scr 3:345
Black, Fred Dixon W49 250
Black, John I. W49 250
Black, Mary S. Geu 221
Black, Richard M. L53 Alpha
L55 57; L57 Alpha
L59 Alpha; L60 Alpha
Black, Robert W. N70 499
Black, Stella Whi 567
Blackburn, John L. Ban 167
Blackham, Sarah Ann Whi 549
Blackstock, Edward J.
N70 464
Blackwell, William L.
Scr 3:328
Blad, Addie Minerva Hamblin
Mea 104
Blad, Anders Gustaf Mea 101
Blad, Angus G. N70 279
W49 250
Blad, Angus Gustavus Mea 102
Blad, Carl Levi Mea 103
Blad, Mina Albertina Andersen
Mea 102
Blagg, Caswell Dee N70 274
Blair, A.J. Moh 37
Blair, George G. Ang 662
Blair, John W. Dav 1127
Blair, Minnie Nichols
Ame 351
Blair, Minnie Pauline Nichols
N70 248
Blair, Priscilla Whi 322
Blair, William H. N70 466
Blaisdell, Leonard E.
W49 250
Blake, Edward Wre 431
Blake, Frank A. Wre 590
Blake, George Alexander
Hamilton Chu 1
Blakely, James M. W49 251
Blakely, John McKenzie
W49 251

Blakemore, Richard E.
A82 93; A83 94
L73 xiv; L75 xxiv
L77 xxi; L79 xxii
L81 xxv; L83 xxviii
Blakemore, Richard Eugene
N70 1000
Blaker, Stella M. Mid 98
Blakeslee, L.A. N10 (70)
Blakey, Richard W. W49 251
Blanchard, Beau Gra 69
Blasdel, Henry G. Chr 16
Blasdel, Henry Goode Myl 13
N59 2
Blaud, Elma Sophia Phi 28
Bleak, Charles E. N70 387
Bleak, Nelson C. L57 Alpha
L59 Alpha; L60 Alpha
L61 Alpha
Blennerhassett, E Ang 460
Bliss, _____ Lam 221
Bliss, Horace Greely N24 36
Bliss, Wayne A. N70 808
Blohm, Ethel (Forsythe)
W49 251
Blohm, Walter N. W49 251
Bloisi, Carmelo N24 38
Blosser, Theodore L. N70 389
Blossom, John Ansel Ang 471
Ban 268
Blum, John W. L51 Alpha
Blumdell, Alfred Dav 1128
Blume, Lloyd L. Lam 221
Blumenthal, Louis L. Dav 1100
Blundell, Alfred W31 12
Boak, C.C. L47 Alpha
L49 Alpha; L51 Alpha
W49 25
Boak, Cada C. W07 229
Boardman, H.M. Moh 26
Boardman, Horace P. Scr 2:262
Boardman, Horace Prentiss
W49 251
Boardman, W.M. Jud (6)
Bobay, Jack Phi 29
Boerlin, Henry Scr 3:249
Bogaert, Bruce R. A83 181
A85 183; L83 liv
L85 liv
Bogart, O.H. M78 54
Bogart, Robert D. M78 65
Boggio, Joseph M., Sr.
N70 538
Boggio, Stefano (Steve)
N70 436
Boggs, Benjamin F. Scr 3:407
Boggs, Jane F. Scr 3:15
Boggs, Orren C. Scr 3:15
Bohlman, Robert Lincoln
W49 252
Boldra, Helen Coverston
W49 252

| | | | |
|---|---|---|---|
| Brotherton, Frank | N70 | 961 | |
| Brougher, Wilson | Dav | 1133 | |
| | Wre | 372 | |
| Brown, Adams Franklin | | | |
| | Dav | 1116 | |
| Brown, Alden H. | W07 | 164 | |
| Brown, B. Mahlon | L51 | Alpha | |
| L53 Alpha; L55 | 57 | |
| L57 Alpha; L59 | Alpha | |
| L60 Alpha; L61 | Alpha | |
| L63 Alpha; L73 | xiv | |
| L75 | xxiv | |
| Brown, Carrie M. | W49 | 257 | |
| Brown, Charles LeRoy | Rei | 89 | |
| Brown, D.L. | Wre | 449 | |
| Brown, Edward | Dav | 1117 | |
| Brown, Ernest S. | Chr | 16 | |
| Scr 2:159; W49 | 257 | |
| Brown, George S. | Dav | 1074 | |
| Lab | 22; Scr | 2:60 | |
| W31 | 14; Wre | 700 | |
| Brown, George Samson | O'B | 87 | |
| Brown, Grace Mary | Cur | 57 | |
| Brown, Henry Alexander | | | |
| | Dav | 1088 | |
| Brown, Horace J. | Scr | 2:148 | |
| | M32 | 63 | |
| Brown, Howard | W49 | 257 | |
| Brown, Hugh H. | W07 | 68 | |
| | M15 | (1:27) | |
| Brown, Hugh Henry | Dav | 1089 | |
| | O'B | 88 | |
| Brown, Jim | Gil | 3 | |
| Brown, John P. | Ang | 367 | |
| Brown, Merwyn H. | M50 | 60 | |
| Ros | 65; W31 | 14 | |
| | W49 | 258 | |
| Brown, Merwyn Harold | Cur | 56 | |
| | N70 | 1028 | |
| Brown, Norman D. | N70 | 962 | |
| Brown, Peleg | Dav | 1133 | |
| Brown, Roy Everett | N70 | 892 | |
| Brown, Theodore N. (Kip) | | | |
| | W49 | 258 | |
| Brown, W. Dean | Phi | 29 | |
| Brown, William E. | Dav | 1134 | |
| Brown, William H. | W49 | 258 | |
| Browne, Howard, Jr. | N70 | 623 | |
| Browne, Howard E. | W31 | 14 | |
| | W49 | 258 | |
| Broy, C.L. | Wre | 621 | |
| Bruce, Daniel Eldred | N24 | 47 | |
| Bruce, Floyd H. | Dav | 1134 | |
| Bruce, Harry L. | W49 | 259 | |
| Bruce, Lillian | W49 | 259 | |
| Bruner, Bill | Bru | 35 | |
| Bruno, Anthony, Jr. | Whi | 611 | |
| Brush, John Tomlinson | | | |
| | Suc | 151 | |
| Brust, Pete Mitchell | N70 | 418 | |
| Brutoa, Doctor | Bru | 18 | |

| | | | |
|---|---|---|---|
| Bryan, Charles H. | Goo | 70 | |
| | O'B | 59 | |
| Bryan, James R. | Scr | 2:452 | |
| Bryan, Oscar W. | W49 | 259 | |
| Bryan, Richard H. | A85 | 232 | |
| L73 | xv; L75 | xxv | |
| | L77 | xxi | |
| Bryan, Vernon F. | N70 | 886 | |
| Bryant, Tom | Lam | 225 | |
| Bryner, Casper Franklin | | | |
| | Whi | 341 | |
| Bryson, George Charles | | | |
| | W31 | 14 | |
| Buck, Everett Nathaniel | | | |
| | N24 | 48 | |
| Buckingham, Dwight M. | | | |
| | Scr | 3:392 | |
| Buckingham, F.C. | L57 | Alpha | |
| L59 Alpha; L60 | Alpha | |
| | L61 | Alpha | |
| Buckland, Samuel S. | Ang | 493 | |
| Ban | 209; Chu | 2 | |
| Buckle, Charles | Wre | 580 | |
| Buckles, Oren | Lam | 225 | |
| Bucknell, R.H., Jr. | Cro | 24 | |
| Budelman, H.D. | L47 | Alpha | |
| L49 Alpha; L51 | Alpha | |
| Budelman, Herman D. | W49 | 21 | |
| Buel, David T. | Goo | 132 | |
| Buffington, J.M. | M78 | 45 | |
| Buffington, John M. | M88 | 28 | |
| Bulasky, Solomon | W49 | 259 | |
| Bulette, Clarence E. | Scr | 3:395 | |
| Bullers, Frederick | N24 | 49 | |
| Bulmer, Halbert B. | Scr | 3:129 | |
| Bulmer, Richard A. | Scr | 3:129 | |
| Bulmer, Roscoe Carlyle | | | |
| | N24 | 50 | |
| Bunch, John H. | N70 | 270 | |
| Bunker, Berkeley L. | W49 | 259 | |
| Bunker, Birdie | Arr | 62 | |
| Bunker, Edward | Arr | 46 | |
| Bunker, Vernon E. | L59 | Alpha | |
| L60 Alpha; L61 | Alpha | |
| | L63 | Alpha | |
| Bunker, Berkeley Lloyd | | | |
| | Chr | 16 | |
| Bunker, William M. | M78 | 56 | |
| Bunkowski, August | N70 | 865 | |
| Bunten, John W. | Phi | 29 | |
| Buol, Frank A. | L49 | Alpha | |
| L51 Alpha; W49 | 25 | |
| Buol, Mary | Scr | 3:84 | |
| Buol, Peter | D15 | (11) | |
| | Dav | 1134 | |
| Burch, Henry R. | N70 | 977 | |
| Burdick, Marie W. | Cur | 78 | |
| Burdick, Ralph H. | Cur | 82 | |
| | Scr | 3:403 | |
| Burdick, Truman Adelbert | | | |
| | Wre | 607 | |
| Burgess, Aggie | Whi | 380 | |

```
Campbell, Allen Green                     Carlson, Clifford A.  L47 Alpha
                      Goo    289          Carlson, Frances Catherine
Campbell, Archie Sutherland                                     W49    263
                      N24     55          Carlson, Henry G.    L53 Alpha
Campbell, Aubrey F.  Scr 3:373                L55    64; L57 Alpha
Campbell, Frank      Dav   1086           Carlson, Leonard F.  N70    939
          Scr 2:183; W31     15           Carlson, Norman K.   Rei    155
                      W49    262          Carney, Stephen Woodrow
Campbell, George A. M15 (1:21)                                  W49    263
                      Scr 2:181           Carothers, Virginia Josephine
Campbell, George M.  N70    642                                 Geu    172
Campbell, Horace P.  Scr 2:459            Carpenter, Albert J. Dav   1086
Campbell, J.L.       Ang    500           Carpenter, Charles C.
Campbell, Jack       Phi     31                     N70    560; Scr  3:15
Campbell, James J.   Lam    227           Carpenter, Charles R.
Campbell, John H.    W49    262                                 N70    452
Campbell, Louis G.   O'B     89           Carpenter, David L.  Scr  3:19
Campbell, Louis Graham                    Carpenter, Jay A.    W31     16
                      Ros     49          Carpenter, Jay Arnold
Campbell, Nancy M.   Scr 3:373                                  W49    263
Campbell, Robert L.  N70    605           Carpenter, John C.   N70    515
Campbell, Thomas A.  W49    262           Carpenter, Kenneth R.
Campton, Aaron Denio Dav   1085                                 N70    936
Canavan, Andrew Joseph                    Carpenter, L.N.      Dav   1087
                      Wre    684                                Wre    601
Canepa, William      N70    986           Carpenter, Laura Helm
Canfield, Fred E.    Ang    300                                 N70    999
Cann, Dorothy        W49    262           Carpenter, Luman N.  Scr  2:88
Cann, E. Beale       N70    314           Carpenter, Marvin H. N24     57
Cann, Mrs. Edna Beale                     Carpenter, William W.
                      Cur     93                                Scr  2:90
Cann, Eli  Cur    91; O'B     89          Carr, George A.      Scr 2:384
Cann, Eli E.         W49    262           Carr, George Augustus
Cannan, James Clyde  W49    262                                 W49    264
Cannon, Howard W.    Cro     28           Carr, Margery McKnight
Cannon, Howard Walter                                           Phi     31
                      Chr     16          Carrigan, Chester C. (Chet)
Cannon, Vernon K.    N70   1045                                 W49    264
Cantlon, Edward      Scr 2:469            Carrington, Carroll C.
Cantlon, Edwin L.    W49    263                                 W49    264
Cantlon, Frank       Scr 2:468            Carruthers, L.G.     L57 Alpha
Cantlon, Vernon      W49    263           Carson, James        Lam    228
Cantwell, Charles A. O'B     89           Carson, Kit          Ban     45
          W31    16; W49    263           Carter, Allen B.     W49    264
Capell, W.R.         Wre    582           Carter, Arthur Nelson
Capriola, Joseph M.  Lam    227                     N70    375; Whi    268
Captain Truckee      Tay     69           Carter, Austin Turnbow
Capucci, Willie      N70    249                                 Whi    363
Capurro, Joe         N70    885           Carter, Charles V.   W31     16
Capurro, Louis J., Jr.                    Carter, Henry Lafayette
          L47 Alpha; L49 Alpha                                  Whi    354
          L51 Alpha; W49     25           Carter, Herbert E.   Scr 3:463
Capurro, Randall V.  L73    xxix          Carter, Herbert Earl N70    870
Carden, A.B.         Lam    227           Carter, James Utley  Whi    356
Cardinal, Joseph A.  Cur    154           Carter, Mrs. Jessie G.
Cardinal, Leo H.     N70    837                                 Cur     37
Carling, John        Ang    494           Carter, Paul R.      W49    264
Carlsen, Alvin P.    N24     56           Carter, Philip J.    Whi    271
Carlson, Charles Alfred                   Carter, Robert E.    W49    265
                      Ros     67          Carter, Robert Ford  N24     58
Carlson, Charles Alfred, Jr.              Carter, Samuel Utley Whi    312
                      Cur    105          Carter, Vera         Whi    394
```

Carter, William S.    Scr  3:264
Cartwright, Andrew J.
                      Dav  1087
Carver, Gerald M.     N70   953
Carville, Edward, Jr.
                      L51  Alpha
Carville, Edward D.   W49   265
Carville, Edward P.   O'B    89
            Scr 2:496; W49   265
Carville, Edward Peter
            Chr   16; Dav  1088
            Myl  107; N59   19
Cary, William M.      Ang   559
Casady, O. Leroy      N70   644
Casazza, Anthony T.   Scr  3:204
Casazza, Joseph P.    Scr  3:205
Casazza, Paul J.      Scr  3:204
Case, Harold          W31    16
Case, Harry           Lam   228
Case, Lee             N70   540
Caserta, John A.      Phi    32
Casey, Ralph Stuart   W49   265
Casey, Walter P., Jr.
                      Cro    30
Casey, Walter Pevar, Jr.
                      N70   286
Cashell, Robert A.    A85   246
            L83  xxv; L85   xxv
Cashill, William John
            M50  136; W49   266
Cashman, James        M50   114
            Scr 3:173; W49   266
Cashman, James, Sr.   Cro    32
Cassels, Bessie       Bru     8
Cassels, Charles      Bru     8
Cassels, Lucy         Bru     8
Cassels, Maggie       Bru     8
Cassidy, George W.    Ang   299
            Goo  348; Scr 1:325
Cassidy, George William
                      Chr    16
Cassidy, Joseph       Suc   147
Cassinelli, Robert A.
                      N70   455
Castagna, Edwin       W49   266
Castello, Vernon J.   N70   982
Castle, D.A.          L53  Alpha
Castle, Forest R.     Lam   228
Castle, Herbert Udell
                      W31    16
Caston, Henry         Lam   228
Castor, George        Lam   228
Catlett, Russell C.   W49   266
Caton, A.J.           W49   266
Cattermole, R.W.      Scr  2:84
Caughlin, Cornelia    Scr  3:209
Caughlin, William H.  Scr  3:208
                      Wre   539
Cavanaugh, Charles R.
            N70  201; W49   266
Cavanaugh, Dennis     Scr  3:458

Cavanaugh, John E.    L47  Alpha
                      W49   267
Cave, Woodrow Weber   W49   267
Cavell, William H.    Scr  3:98
Cavell, William Henry
                      Wre   746
Caviglia, Thomas J.   N70   335
Cavnar, Peggy         L79   xlvi
Cazier, Harry         Gra    69
Cazier, Henry Hallowell
                      N70   854
Cazier, James A.      N70   327
Cazier, Jefferson D.  Wre   514
Cazier, John H.       Wre   514
Ceander, Anton P.     Dav  1088
Cecchini, Charles     N70   292
Centras, John         Ete    45
Cerasola, W.J.        N70   825
Ceresola, Louis M.    N24    60
Cerfoglio, Fiori D.   N70   886
Cerri, Loui           N70   455
Chachas, John G.      N70   345
Chadburn, Robert Henry
                      Whi   361
Chadwell, William C.  W49   267
Chafey, Elwin S.      Ske   322
Chamberlin, W.R.      Ang   636
Chambers, John K.     Dav  1102
Chambers, John Karr   O'B    89
Chambers, Katherine D.
                      W49   267
Chambers, Riley Robert
                      N70   372
Chambers, Thomas Karr
                      O'B    89
Chandler, Charles S.  Dav  1097
                      O'B    90
Chandler, Roscoe Perry
                      Dav  1099
Chaney, Lonie         A82    20
            A83  121; L75  xxxix
            L79 xlvii; L81 xlviii
                      L83  lviii
Chapin, Nealy H.      Dav  1121
            Scr 3:394; W31    16
Chapman, C.A. "Chappie"
                      Per    50
Chapman, Don S.       L47  Alpha
            L49 Alpha; L51 Alpha
                      W49 26, 267
Chapman, Glen         Lam   228
Chappelle, Mrs. B.F.  Bin   139
Chappelle, Benjamin Franklin
                      W49   267
Charles, Frank        Lam   228
Chartz, Alfred        O'B    90
Chartz, Alfred J.     Scr  2:333
Chartz, Alfred Jean   Wre   509
Chartz, John M.       Scr  2:335
Chartz, John Macgregor
                      O'B    90
Chartz, Karl W.       N24    61

13

Chase, Frank J.          D15   (15)
                         Scr  3:131
Chatwin, Hollis E.       W49    268
Cheminant, Alexis S.     M88     35
Cheney, Azro E.          M15  (1:35)
              Scr 2:113; Wre    549
Cheney, Azro Eugene      Jud    (7)
                         O'B     91
Cheney, E.W.             Scr  2:115
Cheney, Everett W.       O'B     91
Cheney, James Hiram      Dav   1112
Cheney, Minor Eugene     Dav   1113
Cheney, Raymond Stewart
                         Dav   1113
Chernick, Eugene B.      N70    503
Chesley, J.G.            Moh     45
Chesnut, Isabella Smith
                         Whi    359
Chessher, Hubert Byrd
                         W49    268
Chester, Charles Henry
                         N70    591
Chester, Ray             Lam    229
Chevallier, Pete         Hal    121
                         Lam    229
Chevallier, Pete E.      N70    485
Chiatovich, Cecil L.     Scr  3:211
Chiatovich, John         Esm     29
                         Ete    112
Chiatovich, Stanley Martin
                         N70    299
Chichester, Bruce H.     Scr  3:348
Chielovich, Elia         Ete    142
Child, John S.           Ang    382
                         Ban     88
Chism, Mrs. Alice A.     Bin    139
Chism, Edward W.         Scr   2:49
Chism, Edward Warren     M50    142
                         W49    268
Chism, Gardner           Dav   1113
              Scr 2:47;  Wre    604
Chism, Harry C.          Scr   2:50
Chism, John              Scr   2:48
Chism, John H.           W49    268
Chiucovich, Peter        Ete    142
Christ, Herman C.        W49    268
Christensen, Chester S.
         L49 Alpha; L51 Alpha
         L53 Alpha; L55     65
         L57 Alpha; L59 Alpha
         L60 Alpha; L61 Alpha
         L63 Alpha; L75 xxxix
                         W49     26
Christensen, M.J.        L53 Alpha
         L55     65; L57 Alpha
         L59 Alpha; L60 Alpha
Christensen, Marcus J.
                         Arr     63
Christensen, Marie       Whi    616
Christensen, Peter       N70    601
Christensen, Soren C.
                         Whi    608

Christian, John W. "J",Sr.
                         N70    256
Christian, W.W.          Bru     24
Christian, Walter M.     Cur    150
Christofforsen, Anna     Whi    618
Church, Frank M.         Dav   1077
Church, James E.         Scr  2:112
                         Tay    151
Church, James Edward     W31     17
                         W49    269
Churchyard, Wendell H.
                 Ros    54; Scr 3:306
Ciliax, Edgar D.         W49    269
Cirac, "Grandfather"     Bru      9
Cirac, Louis             Bru      8
Cirac, Marie             Bru      8
Cislini, Angelo          Bru     14
Cislini, Billy           Bru 14,  29
Cislini, Frank           Bru     14
Cislini, Giacomina       Bru     14
Cladianos, Pete          W49    269
Clagget, William H.      O'B     63
Clagget, William M.      Goo    137
Claiborne, Harry         L49 Alpha
Claiborne, Harry E.
                       W49 26,  269
Claiborne, Paul          Bix     43
Clancy, Patrick Hugh     N24     64
Clapp, E.W.              N10  (176)
Clapp, Hannah Keziah     Geu      1
              N07   58;  Tay     57
Clark, Ann               Whi    352
Clark, Charles R. (Pat)
                         W49    269
Clark, Mrs. Euphenia     Bin    139
Clark, Fred M.           Dav   1078
Clark, H.H.              Suc    128
Clark, J.S. (Jack)       W31     17
Clark, Jacob L.          Scr  2:422
Clark, James             Wre    458
Clark, Lincoln Grant     Wre    407
Clark, Marguerite Gosse
                         W31     17
Clark, Nina              W49    270
Clark, Orvy Walter       N70    250
Clark, Sarah E.          Per    134
Clark, Theodore W.       Cur     35
                         Per    135
Clark, W.H.              D07   (17)
                         W07    122
Clark, Walter E.         M32     11
              Scr  3:12; W31     17
Clark, Walter Ernest     W49    270
Clark, Walter Van Tilburg
                         W49    270
Clark, Wilbur            Cro     34
Clark, William A., Jr.
                         Scr   3:13
Clarke, John P.          N70    596
Clarke, John Robb        W31     17
Clarke, Samuel Tracy     W49    270
Clarno, Herbert S.       N70   1038

14

Class, Alton Earle        Mid     49
Class, F.E.               Mid     49
Claudio, Thomas M.        N24     62
Clawson, Jack H.          W49    271
Clay, Thos. L.            N70    410
Clayton, Joshua           Goo    236
Cleary, Charles W., Jr.
                          N70   1044
Cleary, J. Joseph         W49    271
Cleaver, Kimber           Ang    499
Cleghorn, John            D07    (21)
Clemens, Samuel           N09     40
Clemens, Samuel L.        Goo    250
Clemons, Jay              Scr  3:108
Cleveland, A.C.           Goo    293
Cleveland, Abner C.       Scr  2:103
Cleveland, Abner Coburn
                      Ang  Facing 189
Cliff, Frank              Scr  2:362
Cliff, Samuel             Scr  2:361
                          Was    102
Cline, Bertha Aubrey Manhire
                          N70    192
Cline, Vasie              N70   1040
Clinedinst, Mrs. Lillie
      Barbour             Bin    139
Clingermann, George H.
                          N70    270
Clokey, Ira Waddell       Rei    131
Close, Melvin D., Jr.
      A82      95; L73     xv
      L75     xxv; L77    xxii
      L79    xxiii; L81   xxvi
Clough, Charles E.        M32    107
Cloward, Albert           Whi    566
Clubine, Charles          Lam    229
Clubine, Charles W.       Scr  3:495
Clyde, Elbert T.          Scr  2:345
Cobb, Charles L.          N10   (158)
Cobb, Lamar               N70    966
Cobb, William A.          Wre    533
Cobeaga, Miguel           Sil    414
Cochran, Chester Lee      Ros     78
Codd, A.A.                D15    (13)
      N10    (74); W07    138
Codd, Arthur A.           M15  (1:59)
Codd, Arthur Ashton       Dav   1078
Coddington, Francis J.
                          W49    271
Coe, Joe                  Bru     22
Coe, Lawrence             Bru     22
Coffin, Blaine            Lam    230
Coffin, Bob               A83    127
      A85     129; L83    lxix
                          L85     lv
Coffin, Golden            Lam    230
Coffin, Trenmor           Ang    544
      Ros      31; Scr   2:54
                          Wre    429
Coffin-Summerfield, Marie
      Louise              Cur     19

Cohen, Alfred             O'B     91
Cohen, Joe M.             W49    271
Cohen, Michael            Dav   1120
Cohen, Paul               Phi     32
Cohen, Sidney Bert        Wre    436
Cohn, Felice              Bin    140
      O'B      91; W31     18
                          W49    271
Cohn, Louis J.            W31     18
Coit, Howard              M78     46
Coitt, Howard             M88     32
Colbath, Alex.            D07    (20)
Colburn, R.L. (Dick)      D07    (14)
Colburn, Richard Lincoln
                          Suc    109
Colcord, R.K.            W07     38
Colcord, Roswell K.       Chr     16
      Dav    1114; N59      8
                          Wre    338
Colcord, Roswell Keyes
      Myl      49; Scr  1:363
                          Scr   2:80
Cole, A.M.                Wre    732
Cole, George A.       M15 (1:111)
Cole, Thomas              M78     49
Cole, Wayne               L49  Alpha
                          W49     26
Cole, William             Lam    230
Coleman, B.W.             Dav   1261
Coleman, Benjamin W.      O'B     91
      Ros      43; Scr   3:96
                          W31     18
Coleman, Dave             Scr  2:458
Coleman, George P.        Cur    158
                          Ros     68
Coleman, John W.          M78     72
Coll, Daniel              Dav   1115
Collett, George Arthur
                          Doc    154
Collett, Hugh             Doc    159
Collingwood, DeVere C.
                          N70   1010
Collins, Edward R.        Dav   1164
Collins, Eugene (Gene)
      A83     118; A85    120
      L83      lx; L85    lvi
Collins, Joe              L57  Alpha
      L59  Alpha; L60  Alpha
Collins, Thomas F.        Cro     36
Colton, Gordon            N70    364
Colucci, Michele          N24     65
Colyer, Marvin E.         N70    527
Combs, Wiley              Lam    230
Comerford, James          Wre    711
Coming, James William
                          Phi     33
Comins, Henry A.          Ang    659
      Dav    1114; Moh     36
Compston, George Elwood
                          N70    870
Compston, James, Sr.      N70    991

15

Comstock, Henry Tompkins
    Paige             N09    69
                        Scr 2:441
Comstock, Kiler K.    Scr 3:427
Conboie, Joseph A.    Wre   356
Condie, Rose Marie Austin
                        N70   208
Conelly, Allen E.     N70   578
Conelly, Mabel Anne Finley
                        N70   580
Conley, Clarence      Lam   230
Conlon, John F.       Cro    38
Connell, M.O. (Mike)  Lam   231
Connell, Virgil S.    Scr 3:203
Conner, Verlita       Phi    33
Connolly, Tim         Dav 1164
Connor, Charles L.    N70   238
Connor, James E.     D07  (16)
Connor, P.E.         Goo   265
Connor, Patrick Edward
                        Chu     5
Connor, R.H.        Lam   231
Conrad, Earl         Lam   231
Conrad, Harry       Lam   231
Conrad, Jacob       Lam   231
Considine, John Lyons
                        Wre   440
Converse, Edmund     Cro    40
                        W49   272
Conway, K.J.        Wre   638
Conway, Nelson Harlin
                        W49   272
Conway, P.J.        Scr 2:363
Cook, Eliza          Geu    92
Cook, Emmett W.      W49   272
Cook, F.W.          N10  (96)
Cook, Frederick William
                        Cur    25
Cook, Harry D.       Geo   345
Cook, John S.        D07  (13)
Cook, Samuel         Lam   232
Cook, Wally          Esm    37
Cooke, H.R.         W31    18
Cooke, Herman R.     Dav 1164
                        Wre   654
Cooke, Herman Richard
         O'B   92; W49   272
Cooke, Hermon R.     Scr 2:137
Cooley, Elton        W31    19
Cooney, William M., Jr.
                        N70   561
Cooper, Annie Johnson
                        W49   272
Cooper, Bert L.      Phi    33
Cooper, Clum         N70   888
Cooper, Geraldine E. N70   886
Cooper, Henry       N24    66
Cooper, John Corneilus
                        N24    68
Cooper, William H.    Dav 1165
Copenhaver, Roxie    N70   483
Coppersmith, William Wre   329

Corbett, Christie (Anderson)
    Thompson      W49   272
Corbett, Roger      W49   273
Cord, E.L.          L57 Alpha
Cordes, Chris J.      N70   844
Cordes, Fred         Dav 1165
Corlett, James L.     N70   580
Cornelius, Leslie Edgar
                        N70   584
Cornell, John H.      Scr 2:465
Cornell, Robert Hamilton
                        N70   549
Cornwall, C. Norman  W49   273
Corta, Florencio     Sil   319
Corta, Henry J.      N70   497
Corta, Pedro         Sil   313
Cory, Calvin M.      W49   273
Coschina, Martin     Ete   106
Cosens, Karl Wesley  N70   820
Costa, A. Tony       N70   560
Cotant, William      Lam   232
Cottinger, William    Lam   232
Cottrell, George W. Shutter
                        Wre   561
Cottrell, William D. Wre   719
Couch, Glenn P., Jr. N70   435
Coughlin, Joseph John
                        Dav 1165
Coulson, Celestia Brace
                        W49   274
Coulter, Steven A.    A82    22
        L75   xl; L77 xxxvii
        L79 xlviii; L81 xlix
Coulthard, G. William
        L51 Alpha; L53 Alpha
                        W49   274
Coverston, George C. N70   342
          Scr 3:259; W31    19
Coverston, George Cleveland
                        W49   274
Covington, Herbert L.
                        L53 Alpha
Cowan, Alexander    Ban   171
                        Was   217
Cowan, Leon D.       Phi    34
Cowen, H.D.          D07  (22)
Cowden, Joel B.      Scr 2:502
Cowgill, Thomas Washington
                        Rei    73
Cowing, George W.    Dav 1166
Cowles, Mrs. Emma E. Hammond
                        Cur    50
Cowles, Richard H.    M32    93
                        Scr 2:270
Cowles, Richard Hart Ros    80
Cowles, Robert I.     N70   626
Cox, Clyde Carson    Cro    42
Cox, Fred Gilbert    Suc   115
Cox, Ollie           Lam   232
Cox, Ramsey M.       M15 (1:49)
Cox, Walter          L47 Alpha
Cox, Walter J.        W49   274

Cox, William L.        Wre    370
Cozzalio, Alexander A.
                      Scr  2:225
Cozzalio, Alexander Andrew
                      W49    274
Craddock, Robert Glen
        A82    24; A83   160
        A85   162; L73   xxix
        L75    xl; L77  xxxvii
        L79 xlviii; L81  xlix
        L83   lxi; L85   lvii
Cradlebaugh, John      Chr     17
Cragin, Ernest W.      Scr  3:179
                      W49    274
Craig, John S.         Ang    420
                      Wre    504
Craig, Lois            Cro     44
Craig, W.J.            D07    (19)
Crain, Clarence S.     Dav   1166
                      M15  (2:47)
Crain, Mary Helen      N70    190
Craise, Mr.            Wre    590
Crampton, Eugene R.    Dav   1079
Crandall, Robert Ashley
                      W49    275
Crane, Ervin           Ang    632
Crane, James A.        N70    256
Crane, James M.        Scr  1:127
Crane, W.T.            Ang    391
Craven, Thomas O.      Jud    (25)
Craven, Thomas Owen    W49    275
Crawford, Cranford L., Jr.
                      L73    xxx
Crawford, Don          L47  Alpha
        L49 Alpha; L51 Alpha
        L53 Alpha; L55    65
        L57 Alpha; L59 Alpha
        L60 Alpha; L61 Alpha
                      W49     26
Crawford, Don Carlos   W49    275
Crawford, James        Moh     15
Crawford, Oliver Princeton
                      Moh     40
Creel, Cecil W.        Scr  3:188
                      W31     19
Creel, Cecil Willis    W49    275
Creel, Lorenzo D.      Scr  3:187
Crescenzo, Samuel      Wre    333
Cresswell, H.T.        Moh     45
Creveling, Earl Lamonte
                      W49    275
Creveling, Earle L.    Scr  2:155
Crider, Rex Arlo       Scr  2:247
Crisler, Clara M.      Scr  3:100
                      W49    276
Crisler, William H.    Scr   3:99
Crocker, Alvan W.      Wre    410
Crockett, James R.     Cro     46
Crockett, John         M88     28
Crockett, L.L.         Moh     13
Crockett, Lyman L.
     Ang  Facing 76; Scr  2:391

Crofut, Frederick B. Scr  3:319
Cromer, Lawrence Washington
                      Wre    641
Cronant, C.H.          Wre    713
Crosby, David          Ang    597
                      Wre    565
Crosby, Fred M.        N70    888
Crosby, George T.      Scr  2:390
Crosby, Molanthin Dewey
                      N70    277
Crosby, Paul Thomas    N70    849
Crosby, Ray A.         L60  Alpha
Cross, Archie L.       L49  Alpha
        L51 Alpha; W49     26
Crossen, Vernon        N24     70
Crossman, James H.     M88     34
Crosson, Jane Elizabeth
                      Geu     51
Crowell, J. Irving, Jr.
                      N70   1021
Crowell, Royal D.      W49    276
Crowell, Royal Davis   Ros     87
Crowell, William J.    W49    276
Crows, Archie L.       Scr  3:499
Crumley, J. Grant      Scr  3:139
        W31    19; M32    137
Crumley, Newton        W31     20
Crumley, Newton H.     L55     58
        L57 Alpha; W49    276
Crumley, Newton Hunt N70    872
Cuddy, William Thomas
                      Dav   1079
Culberson, A.P.        Lam    232
Culbert, W. Gerald     W49    276
Culbertson, David Edward
                      W49    276
Culbertson, Harry W.   Dav   1108
Culley, Clem Lloyd     N70    381
Culp, George Bun       N24     72
Culverwell, Charles    Scr  3:520
                      W49    277
Culverwell, Jennie W.W.
                      W49    277
Culverwell, Jennie Wadsworth
     Wilcox            Mea    111
Cunningham, Benjamin Dav   1109
Cunningham, Francis J.
        W31    20; W49    277
Cunningham, Jack B.    W49    277
Cunningham, John R.    Dav   1119
Curieux, Jennie A.     Geu    219
Curler, B.F., Jr.      Jud     (8)
Curler, Benjamin       Ang    521
        Dav  1120; O'B     93
                      Wre    600
Curler, Benjamin F.    Wre    342
Curler, Benjamin Franklin
                      O'B     92
Curnow, James          Dav   1167
Currie, John Curis     Ros      2
Curry, Abraham         Tay     89
Curtin, William H.     Scr  2:302

17

Curtis, Allen A.
    Ang     Facing 468
Curtis, Blaine C.        N70     251
Curtis, James H.         Scr     3:279
Curtis, Loren B.         W07     176
Curto, Leo L.            W49     277
Cushing, Fred A.         Dav     1207
Cushman, Elizabeth       Scr     2:450
Cushman, J.J.            Ang     368
Cushman, James B.        Scr     2:459
Custer, Oliver Cole      W49     278
Cuthbertson, A.A.,       N70     494
Cutler, James G.         Suc     141
Cutting, H.C.            Haw     18
Cutting, Henry Colman
                         Dav     1202
Cutts, Charles F.        Scr     3:91
Cutts, Charles Francis
                         Ros     56
Czykowski, John          N70     847


DaCosta, Albert R.       W31     20
Daggett, R.M.            Moh     58
Daggett, Rollin M.       Goo     185
                         Scr     1:308
Daggett, Rollin Mallory
    Ang     321; Chr     17
                         Lew     11
Dahl, B.F.               M88     33
Dahl, Carlyn Roth        Phi     62
Dahl, Paul Edward        Phi     62
Dailey, George Samuel
                         N24     73
Dakin, Elijah            Lam     232
Dakin, Elmer             Lam     232
Dakin, Judson            Lam     233
Dakin, Steven            Lam     234
Dakin, William (Bill)
                         Lam     234
Dalbey, Gladys H.        W49     278
Dale, George Whitefield
                         Wre     679
Dall, John H.            Was     151
Dallas, Donald Martin
                         Phi     34
Dalton, Peter            Wre     637
Dalton, Thomas H.        Wre     661
Daly, James H.           O'B     93
Daly, Joseph L., Jr.     W49     278
Daly, Marcus             Goo     270
Daly, S.W. "Zeke"        Lam     234
                         N70     552
Damele, John V.          N70     1027
Damm, John G.            W49     278
Dana, Ella Marian        Lam     234
Dangberg, Heinrich Friedrich
                         Geo     286
Dangberg, Henry F., Sr.
                         Scr     3:55

Dangberg, Henry Fred, Jr.
                         N70     1021
Dangberg, Henry Fred, Sr.
    Dav     1255; Wre     359
Dangberg, John B.        W49     278
Dangberg, William        Dav     1195
                         Scr     3:105
Daniel, Fannie           Geu     281
Daniel, Jasper           Ang     421
Daniel, Mrs. Tegwen M.
                         Cur     103
Daniels, Lowell          Scr     3:148
Dann, F.P.               O'B     93
Dann, Fred P.            Dav     1195
D'Arcy, Nicholas         D07     (29)
Darling, Michael         N70     488
Darrough, James          N70     871
Darrough, Laura Stebbins
                         Mur     84
Darrough, Raymond F.     N70     1022
Darrough, William Travis
                         N70     1046
Dat-So-La-Lee            Scr     3:113
                         Tay     129
Davenport, Thomas S.     Moh     53
Davey, John W.           Dav     1196
David, LeRoy             L57     Alpha
David, William M.        Dav     1196
    Ros     41; Scr     2:238
Davidovich, John         Ete     128
Davidovich, Milan        N10     (120)
Davidson, Bertha L.      Phi     35
Davie, Frances Gibson
                         N70     834
Davie, Orrin W.          W31     20
Davin, Amie Frank        N24     74
Davin, John P.           N70     1047
Davis, Blanch M. Ferguson
                         N70     239
Davis, Catherine Kirby
                         Mea     112
Davis, Charles           Mur     302
Davis, Charles Wesley
                         W49     278
Davis, Dana              Phi     35
Davis, "Diamondfield Jack"
                         Suc     121
Davis, Diana Alvina Burger
    Mezger                Geu     187
Davis, Elton Nathaniel Wilsey
                         Dav     1196
Davis, George Lawrence, Jr.
                         N70     206
Davis, George R.         Moh     22
Davis, George Stevens
                         N24     76
Davis, Gerald Wesley     W49     279
Davis, Herman            N10     (12)
    Ros     39; Wre     368
Davis, Howard            Lam     234
Davis, J.R.              Suc     124
Davis, James Bailey      Mea     112

18

Davis, James Clark    Phi    36
Davis, James R.       D07    (27)
          Ske   331; W07    101
Davis, Larry D. "Smokey"
                      Phi    36
Davis, Lee J.         Lab    27
                      O'B    94
Davis, Lute           N24    78
Davis, Morrill W.     Scr  3:163
                      W49    279
Davis, Nan K.         W49    279
Davis, Nellie Verrill
                      Ame    345
Davis, P.E.           Wre    513
Davis, Richard B.     Dav   1175
Davis, Sam            Moh    63
Davis, Sam P.         Ang    314
Davis, Samuel P.      Scr  2:109
                      Wre    418
Davis, Samuel Post
                      Tay  126, 155
Davis, W.L., Jr.      L53  Alpha
Davis, Wesley Lincoln, Jr.
                      W49    279
Davis, William M.     Scr  2:238
Davison, Charles August
                      N24    79
Dawe, William (Bill)  Lam    234
Dawes, E.M.           Scr  2:486
Dawley, A.G.          Wre    468
Dawson, D.A.          Wre    586
Dawson, Edward B.     W31    20
Day, Charles E.       Scr  3:456
Day, George B.        Scr  3:455
Day, James H.         Scr  3:457
Day, John             Lam    234
Day, Sylvester H.     Ang    224
Day, Vane             N70    578
Dayton, Harold Potter
                      W49    279
Dayton, Rueben P.     Moh    33
Deady, Charles L.     Dav   1178
                      M15  (2:71)
Deal, W.E.F.          Ang    585
                      Wre    723
Dean, Flora           G85    1
Dean, Graham Morse    M50    66
Dean, Joe  G85    1; Gra    52
Dean, Walter E.
              Ang  Facing 124
Deane, Coll           M78    37
                      M88    32
Dearing, Charles E.   Scr  3:143
Dearing, Laura Lide   Geu    288
de Arrieta, Joe F.    N70    509
Deas, Henry           M88    28
DeBell, Joseph        Ros    1
De Braga, Francis "Frank"
      Thomas          N70    232
de Braga, Joe         Bru    9
Deck, John H.         Scr  3:443
Deckelman, D.T.       W31    21

Deep Springs John     Esm    2
DeHart, Sonia Barndt  N70   1037
Deidesheimer, Philip  Ban    115
Deidesheimer, Philipp
          Ang  573; Scr  1:276
Dekinder, John        W49    280
Delaney, Ed           L61  Alpha
                      L63  Alpha
Delaney, Edward T.    W49    280
DelCarlo, Gino        N70    912
Del Giudice, Paul J.  Doc    147
                      W49    280
De Lonchant, Felix    Dav   1170
DeLong, Emmet         N70    472
DeLong, William, Jr.  N70   1023
DeLongchamps, Felix   Scr  2:233
de Longchamps, Fred J.
                      M15  (1:79)
DeLongchamps, Fred J.
                      M32    81
de Longchamps, Frederic J.
                      M50    56
DeLongchamps, Frederic J.
                      Scr  2:234
De Longchamps, Frederic Joseph
                      W49    280
DeLongchamps, Philip M.
                      N70    965
De Longchamps, Phillip M.
                      W49    280
Deluca, John J.       W49    280
De Lucchi, John, Mrs.
                      Scr  2:366
Demers, Daniel J.     L73    xxx
      L75   xli; L77 xxxviii
Deming, M.W.          W49    281
Demosthenes, Peter    W49    281
Denney, John E.       N70    418
Denning, Teresa       N70    240
Dennis, John H.       Ang    295
Denson, C.S.          N10    (18)
Denton, Hazel         L53  Alpha
                      L55    66
Denton, Hazel B.      Scr  3:236
Denton, Lloyd C.      N70    387
Depp, Frank H.        N70    838
De Quille, Dan        Chr    25
          Goo  213; Lew    5
DeRuchia, Emerson A.  Scr  2:286
DeSpain, Evan I.      L57  Alpha
          L59 Alpha; L60  Alpha
Detch, Milton M.      D07    (26)
          M15 (1:89); W07    126
Detch, Milton Maynard
                      Suc    126
Dettmer, Leland       N70    251
Devaney, Fred A.      N70    507
Devin, Thomas C.      Chu    5
Devlin, John L.       N70    309
Dewar, Archie J.      N70    402
Dewar, James          Wre    751
Dewey, William P.     M78    61

Dey, Richard V.        Ang    597
Dial, William E.       L59  Alpha
        L60 Alpha; L61  Alpha
        L63 Alpha; W49    281
Dibble, Andrew C.      Scr  3:318
Dibble, N.P.           Lam    235
DiCianno, Girlando     N70    365
Dick, Old              Bru     29
Dick, Papa             Bru     29
Dickensen, Charles Wesley
                       Dav   1170
Dickerson, D.S.        W07     36
Dickerson, Denver S. Chr      17
        N10 (144); Scr 1:437
Dickerson, Denver Sylvester
        Myl    73; N59     12
Dickerson, Harvey Denver
                       W49    281
Dickerson, Una Reilly
        Ame   348; Jud   (28)
Dickey, James R.       W49    281
Dieffendorf, Warren T.
                       Suc    150
Dieleman, Jake W.      L59  Alpha
        L60 Alpha; N70    342
Dieringer, Cook        Bru     29
Dieringer, Ed          Bru      9
Dieringer, Rita        Bru     27
Dietz, F.E.            M88     29
Dietz, Philip E.       W49    281
Di Grazia, Eugene J.   N70    549
Di Grazia, John E.     N70    511
Dimmick, Maud F.T.     Scr  2:209
Dini, Joseph E., Jr.   A82     26
        A83   214; A85    216
        L73 xxxi; L75     xli
        L77 xxxviii; L79 xlix
        L81    1; L83 lxxxiii
                       L85  lviii
Dinius, Myra A. Nelson
                       N70    581
Dinsmore, Sanford C.
        M15 (1:107); Scr  3:71
Dinsmore, Sanford Crosley
                       Rei     75
Diskin, M.A.           Lab     92
        O'B    94; W49    282
Diskin, M.A. (Jack)    W31     21
Diskin, Michael Angelo
        M15 (2:77); M50     38
Diskin, Pat A.         Cro     48
Dittenrieder, Mrs. Laura M.
                       Ban     73
Dixon, Bob             Bru    8-9
Dixon, Ethel           Cur    162
Dixon, Frank W.        Scr  2:395
Dixon, Jonathan Brown
                       O'B     94
Dixon, Lawrence Dale   N70    826
Dixon, Robert T.       Scr  2:499
Dixon, Thomas E.       Scr  3:483
Dixon, Thomas Edward   W49    282

Dixon, Willard         W49    282
Dodge, Carl F.         L59  Alpha
        L60 Alpha; L61  Alpha
        L63 Alpha; L73    xvi
        L75  xxvi; L77   xxii
                       L79   xxiv
Dodge, E.R.            N10    (28)
Dodge, Edmund R.       Ang    441
                       O'B     94
Dodge, George S.       M78     32
Dodson, Edwin S.       Phi     36
Doherty, Frank A.      Dav   1104
Doherty, John (Jack) Francis
                       N24     80
Dohr, Peter            Dav   1104
Dohr, Roland N.        W49    282
Dohrenwend, Charles J.
                       W49    282
Donald, Samuel         Ang    312
Donaldson, Melvin G.   N70    586
Donavan, Edwin F.      Dav   1104
Donnellan, John        D07    (28)
Donnellan, John Tilton
                       W07    140
Donnis, Jerrald J.     W49    283
Donovan, Jerome P.     W49    283
Donovan, William       Scr   2:17
Donovan, William M.    Scr   2:18
                       W49    283
Doolin, Wm.            Moh     61
Doretia, _____        Lam    235
Dormer, J.M.           Ang    298
Dorothy, Dorothy       Cro     50
Dorsa, Steve           Lam    235
Dorsey, Al S.          Lam    235
Dorsey, Eliza Lyon     Hal     70
Dorsey, John M.        Hal     69
                       Lam    235
Dory, Miss             G85      9
Dory, Delbert R.       N70    319
Dory, Ruth Emma        W49    283
Doten, Alf.            Moh     65
        Ang   324; Dav   1105
Doten, Samuel Bradford
                       Rei     71
Dotson, Edwin J.       L55     66
Dotson, Robert R.      N70    334
Dotta, David           N70    393
                       W49    283
Dotta, Emilio          Wre    620
Doty, Guy E.           N70    313
Dougherty, William B.
                       Moh     19
Doughty, James C.      Cur    135
                       Dav   1105
Doughty, James Conrad
                       Ros     38
Douglas, Claude        Bru      8
Douglas, H.C.          Scr  3:118
Douglas, H.C. (Hy)     W31     21
Douglas, J.F.          W07    130
Douglas, Joe           Bru      8

Douglas, Roy               Bru      8
Douglas, W.A.              D07    (24)
Douglass, Robert           N10   (172)
Douglass, Robert Lee       M50     26
Dove, James                Lam    237
Dowlen, Walton E.          D07    (25)
                           Ske    339
Dowler, Lloyd              W49    283
Down, James Henry, Jr.
                           W49    283
Downer, Sylvester Spelman
                           O'B     95
Downey, Mrs. Hattie A.
                           Cur     48
Downs, Art L.              Scr  3:258
Doyle, Mrs. Ella J.  Cur   113
Doyle, George              Scr  3:287
Doyle, Howard S.           M32     75
                           W49    283
Doyle, Phillip Andrew
                           Ros     22
Drabnick, Walter E.        D15    (17)
Drake, Frank               Doc     79
Drakulich, Stanley J.
                           L73    xvi
Draper, Laura Dame         Whi    563
Draper, Martha Jane        Whi    551
Draper, Marvin C.          Scr  3:307
Draper, Stanley J.         Scr  3:292
Draper, W. Clayton         Scr  3:309
Drennon, Ted Edward        W49    284
Dresser, William Oscar
                           Dav   1106
Dressler, Augustus F.
                           Ang    383
Dressler, Fred H.          N70    877
Dressler, Myron Park       N70    875
Dressler, William F.       Dav   1257
                           W31     21
Drew, Allan L.             W31     22
Dreyer, Darrell H.         L73   xxxi
        L75   xlii;        L77  xxxix
Driesbach, Monroe A.       Ang    544
Dromiac, Alexandex         Ete    118
                           M15  (1:7)
Dron, Thomas J.            Dav   1106
Drown, Charles Chester
                           N70    531
Drown, Eugene              Lam    237
Drown, Gordon              Lam    237
Drown, Jennie              Geu    212
Druehl, Ralph L.           W49    284
Drury, Wells               Lew     23
                           Moh     69
Du Bois, _____          Lam    237
DuBois, John B.            A82     28
        A83    106;        A85    108
        L81     li;        L83  lxiii
                           L85    lix
Duborg, C.H.               N10    (62)
Duborg, Christopher H.
                           Scr  2:254

Duccini, Antonio           N70    450
Ducey, John B.             Dav   1255
Ducker, Dollie B.          W49    284
Ducker, Mrs. Dollie B.
                           Cur     55
Ducker, Edward A.          Ros     52
                           Scr   3:95
Ducker, Edward Augustes
                           Lab  107; O'B     95
Duelks, Jack W.            W49    284
Duffill, Albert            Scr  3:478
Duffin, Press W., Jr.
                           L47  Alpha
Duffy, Martin C.           L59  Alpha
        L60 Alpha;         L61  Alpha
Duffy, Martin Charles
                           W49    284
Dufurrena, Alex            N70    277
Dufurrena, Raymond John
                           N70    476
Dugan, G.A.                W31     21
Dugan, James Sampson       W49    284
Dumovich, Milo N.          N24     84
Dunaway, Thomas F.         Dav   1169
Duncan, Byron T.           N70    443
Duncan, Henry              Dav   1179
Duncan, Walter             L57  Alpha
Dungan, Flora              L63  Alpha
Dunkle, Dan W.             Scr  2:386
                           W31     21
Dunkle, Darrell M.         Scr  2:387
Dunkle, Darrell Melville
                           N24     82
Dunlop, John C.            Scr  2:427
Dunn, Frank T.             O'B     95
Dunn, Herbert C.           Wre    443
Dunn, James T.             Wre    345
Dunphy, William            Elk    407
Dunseath, Harry            Scr  2:146
Dupuy, Marcel              Bru     21
Duque, Bertrad             Sil    397
Durbrow, Alfred K.         M88     37
Durenberger, Peter Oliver
                           N24     85
Durham, J.C.               W31     22
Durham, John C.            Dav   1178
        M15 (2:39);        M32     55
                           Scr  2:130
Durkee, Joseph             Scr  2:326
Durkee, Samuel C.          Scr  2:325
Dutchman, The              Lam    237
Dutertre, Louis            Wre    478
Duval, Robert E.           N70    999
Duvall, Marius             W07     82
Dye, Lavina                Whi    588
Dyer, Alex                 Bru      8
Dyer, Duane                Bru      8
Dyer, Ed                   Mur    231
Dyer, Edward A.            L59  Alpha
        L60 Alpha;         L61  Alpha
Dyer, Mrs. Edward A.       Mur    299
Dyer, Edwin S.             N70    292

Ellis, Pearis B.        Scr 3:433
Ellis, Pearis Buckner
                        O'B    96
Ellis, Richard Voris Suc   119
Ellis, Robert C.        W49   287
Ellison, Lyle L.        L55    66
                        N70   545
Ellison, Stanley C.     N70  1003
Ellithorpe, C.H.        N10   (66)
Ellithorpe, William Melvin
                        N24    87
Elmore, George          Wre   725
Elsner, Earl Morgan     N70   580
Elston, Henry Knight    Suc   149
Elston, Roy Melvin      W49   288
Elwell, William H.      Scr  3:23
                        W49   288
Embry, William          L49 Alpha
       L53 Alpha;       L55    67
Embry, William D.       W49    26
Embry, William DeCalb
                        N70  1006
Emery, Herbert Ward     W49   288
Emminger, W.G.          L55    58
Emminger, William Glenn
                        N70   821
Emmons, Chester Vernon
                        W49   288
Enders, Hugo A.         W49   288
Engelmann, George       Rei    31
Englert, Matilda Jane
       "Coosie"         N70   508
Englestead, Van         L47 Alpha
                        L51 Alpha
English, Arthur M.      N70   445
Ennedy, Thomas          Bru     9
Ennor, Mrs. Ruth G.     Cur   137
Epley, John             Lam   238
Epperson, Julian Oliver
                        W49   288
Erickson, Violet Boulding
       Cropley          N70   597
Ericson, Pearl C.       Cur    39
Eriksen, Knud L.        N24    88
Erlach, Joseph W.       Phi    37
Ernst, Clarence A.      N70   509
Ernst, George           Ang   522
Errea, Louis            N70   458
Erro, Manuel            Lam   238
Erro, Pedro             Lam   238
Erway, Albert H.        Ang   408
Esser, Ernst Paul       Dav  1176
Etchart, John M., Jr.
                        N70   444
Etchebarren, Jean       Sil   397
Etchegoyhen, Jerome E.
                        Phi    37
Etcheverrietta, Antonio
       "Tony"           Lam   238
Evans, Alvaro           Wre   354
Evans, Charles B.       Lam   239
Evans, Charles R.       Scr 1:510

Evans, Charles Robley
                        Chr    17
Evans, Gene             L57 Alpha
       L59 Alpha;       L60 Alpha
Evans, J. Buren         Scr 3:513
Evans, J.H.             O'B    96
Evans, John N.          M15 (1:87)
Evans, John Newton      Wre   488
Evans, Karl L.          W49   289
Evans, Morris R.        Ske   253
Evans, Terrell          N70   230
Evans, William "Bill"
                        Lam   239
Eveleth, Alpheus T.     Scr 2:251
       W31    23;       W49   289
Everett, Wayne          N70   925
Ewing, Marion J.        N24    89
Exeter, Hazen           N70   511


Fabri, Peter            W49   289
Fagan, John L.          W07   216
Fair, James G.    Ang   Facing 48
       Ban   135;       Goo   178
       M78    23;       M88    23
                        Scr 1:276
Fair, James Graham      Chr    17
Fairbanks, I.W.         Wre   417
Fairchild, Jerry        A85   105
                        L85    1x
Fairchild, Joseph Depuy
                        Ang   305
Fairchild, M.A.         L47 Alpha
                        L51 Alpha
Fairchild, Mahlon A. W49   289
Fairchild, Mahlon Dickinson
                        Ang   311
Fairchild, Oscar L.C.
                        Ang   295
Fairchild, Theodore T.
       "Tate", Jr.      N70   995
Fairchild, Tracy T.     Ros    64
Fairfax, Charlie        Goo    37
Faiss, Wilbur           A82    99
       A83    49;       L77 xxiii
       L79 xxvi;        L81 xxxiii
                        L83   xxix
Falcke, Lena Rose Giardelli
                        N70  1043
Fall, Sally             Per   134
Fallini, Joseph B.      N70  1045
Fant, John              Cur    87
                        Per    54
Faretto, Leslie L.      N70  1049
Farias, Antone L.       N70   880
Farias, Joe M.          Scr 3:337
Farias, Manuel          N70   981
                        Scr 3:337
Farnsworth, David       W49   289
Farnsworth, Frederick A.
                        Scr 2:411

Flavin, Thelma          Lam    240
Flaws, T.J.A.           Wre    375
Fleming, Charles E.     Rei    101
Fleming, Charles Elliot
                        Ros     84
Fleming, Charles L.     Scr  2:415
Fletcher, A.G.          Wre    692
Fletcher, Emery L.      Dav   1182
Fletcher, F.N.          Scr   2:50
Fletcher, Granville A.
                        Scr  2:442
Fletcher, John          W49    293
Fletcher, Merrill       Scr  2:443
                        Wre    322
Fletcher, Merrill M.    W49    293
Flick, Dixie Lee        Scr  3:360
Flick, Warren J.        Scr  3:358
Flinn, Peter J.         Scr  2:449
Flinspach, William      N70    487
Flippin, Roy B.         N70    316
Flood, James C.         Ang    591
        M78    23; M88     24
Florio, A.C.            Scr   3:47
Florio, Angelo C.       N70    300
Flowers, John Carl "Swede"
                        N70    521
Floyd, Ron E.           N70    357
Flynn, Frank            Lam    240
Flynn, Will             Lam    240
Flynn, William Joseph
                        N24     92
Fodrin, Daniel J.       W49    293
Foged, Lawrence Peter
                        N24     94
Fogg, William Augustus
        Dav  1182; Wre    530
Fogliani, Jack          W49    293
Fogliani, Louis,        Scr  3:442
Foley, Helen A.         A82     30
        A83    54; A85     58
        L81   lii; L83    xxx
                        L85  xxvii
Foley, John P.          L73   xvii
Foley, Roger            Scr   3:28
Foley, Roger D.         W49    294
Foley, Roger T.         O'B     98
                        W49    294
Foley, Roger Thomas     Cro     52
Foley, Thomas L.        Dav   1183
                        O'B     98
Folsom, Ellis J.        L47  Alpha
        L49 Alpha; L51  Alpha
                        W49     27
Folsom, Ellis John      N70    841
Folsom, Gilman N.       Was     99
Folwick, Nina Barrigar Burns
                        N70    983
Fong, Wing              Cro     54
Fong, Wing Gay          N70    223
Foote, George A.        Chu      6
Foote, Joseph Warren    Arr     37

Foote, Margie           L73  xxxii
        L75 xxvii; L77   xxiv
Forbes, George W.       Scr  3:256
Forbes, George West     W49    294
Forbes, William J.      Ang    302
Ford, James F.          W31     24
Ford, James F., Jr.     W49    294
Ford, James G.          Scr  3:452
Ford, James H.          Scr  3:137
Ford, Jean E.           A82    101
        L73 xxxii; L75   xlii
        L79 xxvii; L81   xxix
Ford, Stanley           N70    389
Foreman, Afton Mathews
                        Mea    123
Foreman, Joseph N.      N70    376
Foreman, William J.     W49    294
Forman, Charles         Ang    582
Forman, Samuel D.       Scr   3:45
Forman, William         O'B     98
Forman, William Joel    M50     88
Forster, W.D.           N10   (90)
Forsyth, Belle          Whi    364
Fortier, Quincy E.      W49    294
Foster, Bill            Bru     19
Foster, George A.       Scr  3:301
Foster, James T.        W49    295
Foster, John C.         Scr  3:372
Foster, Kenneth G.      M32     97
                        Scr  2:159
Foster, Mack            Bru     19
Foster, Sidney          Cur     33
Foster, William H.      W49    295
Fouilleul, P.J.         W31     24
Fouilleul, P. Joseph    Scr  3:418
Foulks, J.P.            Moh     48
Fountain, Edgar W.      Cro     56
Fourreuill, Andreu      Sil    320
Foutz, Harold B.        W49    295
Fowler, Leonard Burke
        M15 (2:65); O'B     98
Fowler, Reuben (Bob)    N24     96
Fox, J.J.               Ang    408
Fox, L.T.               Ang    604
Fox, Leonard            N70    983
Fox, Ruth               N70    983
Foy, John Bernard       M32    159
        W31    24; W49    295
Frade, Antone J.        N70    971
Fraiser, James          Lam    240
Frame, James M.         W31     24
Francis, David W.       N70    359
Francis, Ed             Lam    241
Francis, Steven C.      A83    223
        A85   225; L83    lxv
                        L85    lxi
Francis, Walter         Bru      8
Francisco, Joseph       Scr  3:138
Francovich, Samuel B.
                        L51  Alpha
Frandsen, Andrew        Geo    330
                        Scr  2:306

25

Frandsen, Frances       Scr  2:307
Frandsen, Frank M.      Scr  3:63
                        W49   296
Frandsen, Peter         Rei    63
            Scr 2:252;  W31    24
Frank, Myron            W49   296
Frank, Samuel           Scr  3:507
Frank, William J.       L53 Alpha
            L55    58;  L57 Alpha
            L59 Alpha;  L60 Alpha
            L61 Alpha;  L63 Alpha
Frankie, Henry          Lam   241
Franklin, Bertha Hansel
                        Cur   138
Franklin, George, Jr.
                        L57 Alpha
Franklin, George E., Sr.
                        Cro    58
Franklin, George Edward
                        N70   265
Franklin, George Edward, Sr.
                        W49   296
Frankovich, Lee         W49   296
Franks, Dan W.          Scr  3:521
Franks, Daniel William
                        W49   296
Franks, Fred F.         Scr  3:459
Franks, Louis B.        Scr  3:459
Fransway, John          L61 Alpha
                        L63 Alpha
Fransway, John, Jr.     W49   297
Franzman, Mrs. Mary C.
                        Bin   140
Fraser, Gordon M.       Dav  1183
Fraser, Owen            Moh    44
Frasier, Hannah Kent    Geu   105
Frazer, Ray F.          W49   297
Frazer, William H.      Dav  1184
                        Wre   519
Frazier, Bruce          N70   536
Frazier, Maude          Cro    60
            Geu   215;  L51 Alpha
            L53 Alpha;  L55    67
            L57 Alpha;  L59 Alpha
            L60 Alpha;  L61 Alpha
Frazier, Walter E.      N70   466
Fredericks, John F.     Scr  3:361
Free, Wenlock W.        L47 Alpha
Freeman, Merrill Pingree
                        Ros     8
Freeman, William        Dav  1184
Freeman, William J.     N70   966
Frehner, Merle          N70   213
Frehner, Wesley         N70  1048
Freitas, Antonio Lucio
                        N24    99
Fremont, John Charles
                        Rei    27
French, A.              Wre   756
French, Greeley         Wre   697
French, John E.         N70   341

French, Le Roy N.       Dav  1184
                        O'B    98
French, Judge Leroy     Lab    25
Freudenthal, Herman E.
                        Wre   446
Frevert, Allen          Dav  1157
Frevert, Clarence H.    N24   100
Frey, George W.         L47 Alpha
Frey, Joseph            Ang   642
                        Was   105
Frey, Lawrence          Dav  1157
Frey, Lyle L.           N70   478
Fricke, Fred W.         N70   906
Fricke, Frederick       Dav  1158
Fricke, William H.      W49   297
Friedhoff, Mrs. Frances
        Gertrude        Cur   127
Friedman, L.A.          W31    25
Friedman, Louis A.      D15   (19)
                        M15 (1:113)
Frissel, Elmer A.       Dav  1158
Fritchie, William       Doc   164
Frohlich, August C.     Dav  1158
                        Scr  2:357
Frost, Ethel L.         Scr  2:288
Frost, Harry J.         M50   124
                        W49   297
Fry, Leslie Mack        L73 xxxiii
Fryberger, Delbert O.
                        W49   297
Fuetsch, Carl F.        L47 Alpha
        L49 Alpha;  W49 27, 297
Fuller, Alton           W49   297
Fuller, Frank S.        N24   102
Fuller, Harold Wayne    N70   590
Fuller, John A.         W49   298
Fuller, Winford Le Roy
                        Dav  1160
Fullerton, Murray       L57 Alpha
Fulmer, Henry M.        Dav  1159
Fulmer, Jacob H.        Dav  1159
        M15 (1:41);  M32   105
Fulstone, Charles L.
                        Ros    36
Fulstone, Fred M.       N70   992
Fulstone, George H.     Scr  3:326
Fulstone, Henry         Was   101
Fulstone, Mary Hill     Ame   352
Fulstone, Paul Edward
                        N70   906
Fulton, Ivy             Moh    27
Fulton, John A.         Scr  2:397
Fulton, John Allen      W31    25
Fulton, John M.         Dav  1143
        M15 (1:91);  Wre   699
Fulton, Mary A. B.      Scr  2:400
Fulton, Robert L.       Scr  2:398
                        Wre   681
Funk, Edward Daniel     Whi   618
Funk, Irva              Whi   582
Fuss, Frank H.          N70   548
Fuss, Frank Herman      W49   298

26

Fuss, Henry W.          Wre    634

Gabica, Frank           N70    483
Gabica, Santiago        Sil    414
Gabler, Laurence        W49    298
Gabrielli, John E.      Jud    (26)
Gadda, Onorato          N24    104
Gage, Kate              Scr  2:479
Gaillard, M.E.          Elk    398
Galbraith, C. Layton    W49    298
Gallagher, Charles      L53  Alpha
        L55    58; L57  Alpha
        L59 Alpha; L60  Alpha
        L61 Alpha; L63  Alpha
Gallagher, Charles W.
                        Scr  3:320
Gallagher, Ella         Geu     66
Gallagher, J.B.         Moh     20
Gallagher, Joe W.       Scr  3:321
Gallagher, John B.      Ang    409
Gallagher, John H.      Dav   1144
        Scr 2:447; W31     25
Gallagher, Joseph C.    Scr  3:320
Gallagher, Mervin J.    L47  Alpha
        L49 Alpha; N70    907
                        W49     27
Gallagher, Patrick      Wre    590
Gallagher, Patrick J.
                        Scr  3:481
Gallagher, Patrick Joseph
                        W31     25
Gallagher, Thomas H.    Lam    241
Gallagher, W.C.         Cur    111
Gallagher, Walter John
                        N24    106
Gallagher, William C.
        Dav 1144; Scr 2:446
Galli, Peter            N24    108
Gallio, John Benjamin
                        N70    226
Galloway, W.W. "Bill"
                        Cro     62
Gallues, Henry N. (Hank)
                        Mid    176
Galusha, C.H.           Haw     30
Galway, Desma Hall      Rei    133
Gambill, Herbert Nelson
                        W31     26
Gamble, John Robert     Phi     37
Gamble, William         Chu      6
Games, John R.          W49    298
Gandolfo, John Tony     N70   1050
Garaghan, Michael B.    Dav   1144
Garat, John B.          Scr  2:422
Garaventa, Edward John
                        N70    647
Garaventa, Frank L.     Scr  3:46
Garaventa, John         Scr  3:45
Garber, John            O'B     34
Garcia, G.S.            Wre    416

Garcia, Joseph P.       N24    109
Garcia, Leslie F.       N70    838
Gardella, Louie Andrew
                        N70    637
Gardiner, John William Tudor
                        Chu      6
Gardiner, William M.    Scr   2:21
Gardiner, William Munson
        Dav 1145; Lab     20
        M15 (2:45); O'B     99
                        W31     26
Gardner, Alice Brewer
                        Geu    209
Gardner, Amos Berry     Whi    342
Gardner, Claude         Mur    141
Gardner, David Cannon
                        Whi    263
Gardner, George Cannon
                        Whi    364
Gardner, George Montgomery
                        Doc     84
Gardner, Jesse          N70    372
Gardner, Martin         Whi    382
Gardner, Mervin L.      W49    298
Gardner, Milton D.      Whi    271
Gardner, Neil L., Sr.
                        Whi    307
Gardner, Paul K.        Scr  3:393
Gardner, Paul Klinker
                        W49    299
Gardner, Raymond John
                        N70    414
Gardner, Samuel Alonzo
                        Whi    368
Garehime, Jacob W.      N70    363
                        W49    299
Garfinkle, Bud          Phi     38
Garhart, William        Ang    575
Garner, Blanch          Gil     11
Garner, Floyd           Gil     11
Garrecht, Gertrude      Wre    442
Garrecht, Gertrude Lang
                        Geu     25
Garrett, Elton G.M.     W31     26
Garrett, Elton M.       N70    243
Garside, Frank F.       W49    299
Garside, Sherwin Frank
                        W49    299
Gartrell, Roy Lanning
                        N70    579
Garven, Pierre P.       Scr  2:480
                        W31     26
Garvin, Desmond Norwood
                        N70    333
Gascue, John D.         Phi     38
Gashwiler, John W.      M78     35
                        M88     35
Gaskins, Robert M.      N70    272
Gaspari, Caesar John    N70    805
Gaspari, Joseph D.      N70    816
Gassaway, Percy Lee (Pat), Jr.
                        N70    320

Gastanaga, Jose Vincent
                          N70    930
Gastanaga, Lola Jimella
     Harvey               N70    932
Gastanaga, Martin         W49    299
Gaston, Henry H.          Moh     31
Gastonada, Jose           Sil    395
Gates, Byron              Wre    384
Gates, Cora E.            Scr  2:491
Gatten, Frederick L.      W49    300
Gatti, Augustino          N24    110
Gay, Sam  Lab    97; Scr  3:388
Gaynor, John S.           Doc    148
                          N70    197
Gazin, Henry John         W49    300
Gedney, Frank S.          O'B     99
Gee, Albert               Whi    614
Geer, Clara               Geu     41
Gelder, Harriet Sewell Smith
                          W49    300
Gelmstedt, Carl O.        Ros     81
Gemmill, David L.         W49    300
Genesy, Babtiste Joseph
                          Dav   1146
Gennett, Carter           Hal     77
                          Lam    241
Gennette, Joe             Lam    241
Gentry, Edward Samuel
                          Mea    124
Gentry, Mary Davis        Mea    124
Genzel, Henry             Wre    569
George, Isabel Green      N70    807
George, John F.           Scr  3:211
George, Sammy             N24    111
Georgeson, Robert L.      W49    300
Georgeson, Robert W.      W49    301
Georgetta, Clel           Bix     59
Georgetta, Clel E.        Jud    (23)
                          W49    301
Georgetta, Clel Evan      N70    189
Gerber, Claude Edward
                          N70    522
Gerbig, Oscar             Scr  3:410
Gergens, _____          Lam    241
Germain, Joseph L.        W49    301
Gerow, James W.           Scr  2:176
Gerow, James Wiggins      W49    301
Getchell, Noble H.        W31     27
Getchell, Noble Hamilton
              M50   32; W49    301
Getto, Virgil M.          A82    103
              A83   205; A85    207
          L73 xxxiii; L75  xliii
              L79   li; L81    xxx
          L83  lxvi; L85    lxii
Gezelin, Emile J.         Jud    (27)
Ghiglia, Frank P., Jr.
                          N70    862
Gialy, Pete               Lam    241
Giannini, Amadeo Peter
                          Mid     81
Gibbons, L.A.             N10  (128)

Gibbons, Lewis A.    Dav   1146
     M15 (1:39); O'B     99
Gibbs, William B.    Wre    540
Gibbs, William Bennett
                     N70    568
Gibson, E.F.         Moh     29
Gibson, Edmund Richard
     (Hoot)          W49    301
Gibson, Mrs. Eva V.  Cur    145
Gibson, James I.     A82    103
          A83  45; A85     47
          L59 Alpha; L60 Alpha
          L61 Alpha; L63 Alpha
          L73 xviii; L75 xxvii
          L77 xxiv; L79 xxviii
          L81  xxxi; L83  xxxi
                     L85 xxviii
Gibson, Horatio Gates
                     Chu      6
Gibson, Renee C. Noel
                     N70    324
Gibson, Roland H.    W49    302
Gibson, Samuel C.    Dav   1146
          Scr 2:294; Wre    619
Gibson, Thomas R.    Scr  2:295
Gibson, W.D.C.       Moh     29
Gibson, W.R.         W31     27
Gibson, William R.   Scr  2:352
Gibson, William Robert
                     O'B    100
Gidney, Frances M.   Phi     38
Giffen, James B.     N10   (58)
Gifford, Charles     N24    112
Gignoux, Jules E.    Wre    360
Gilberg, Carl        Lam    241
Gilbert, Chester Van Tyler
                     N70    265
Gilbert, Henry R.    W49    302
Gilbert, Mrs. Lida Humphrey
                     W31     27
Gilbreath, Eddie J.  W49    302
Gile, Frank D.       Scr  2:456
Giles, Edwin S.      Scr  3:153
Giles, Edwin Scofield
                     W49    302
Giles, Ruth          Gil     47
Gill, Benjamin       M32    149
Gillan, Bennet A.    Scr  3:300
Gilland, Thomas      Lam    242
Gillies, Donald B.   W07     57
Gillies, Donald Burton
                     Suc    127
Gillis, "Jim"        Goo     90
Gillson, George      Ros     32
                     Scr  2:192
Gillson, Philip Y.   Scr  2:194
Gillson, Philip Young
                     M15 (2:31)
Gillson, Phillip Y.  M32    129
Gilmer, Walter M.    W49    302
Gilmer, Walter Merriweather
                     N70    545

Gilmore, Dallas          Lam    242
Gilmore, Virgle Franklin
                         N70    246
Gingery, Robert W.       W49    302
Ginnocchio, John S.      W49    303
Giomi, John F.           L55     67
          L57 Alpha; L59 Alpha
          L60 Alpha; L61 Alpha
                        L63 Alpha
Ginsburg, Edward         W49    303
Ginsburg, Harry          W49    303
Ginsburg, Leo M.         W49    303
Ginsburg, Sam            W49    303
Giomi, John F.           N70    882
Giorgi, Ugo, Sr.         N70    974
Giroux, David            Wre    675
Giusti, Paul             N70    333
Givens, James G.         Dav   1147
Gladding, Gil            Phi     39
Glaser, Anna Christine Brown
                         Geu     97
Glaser, Arthur           Hal     66
                         Lam    242
Glaser, Christine        Scr   2:99
Glaser, Clarence         Lam    242
Glaser, Dan              Lam    242
Glaser, Darlow           Lam    242
Glaser, George           Hal     56
Glaser, George M.        Lam    242
Glaser, George Mathias
                         N70    567
Glaser, Loren            Lam    243
Glaser, Mathias          Hal     50
          Lam    243; Scr   2:98
Glaser, Norman           Hal     63
                         Lam    243
Glaser, Norman D.        A82    107
          A83     97; L61 Alpha
          L63 Alpha; L77    xxv
          L79    xix; L81 xxxii
                        L83 xxxii
Glaser, Norman Dale      N70   1015
Glaser, Walter           Hal     59
Glaser, Walter A.        Lam    244
Glasmeier, Herman G.     N24    114
Glass, Rev. Joseph S.
                         Gor     25
Gleason, William T.      Dav   1155
Gleason, William Thomas
                         N24    115
Glenn, M.M.              Ang    297
Glidden, Bruce           Dav   1217
Glock, Andrew Martin     N70    966
Glover, Alan H.          A82     32
          A83     91; A85     93
          L73 xxxiv; L75 xliii
          L77 xxxix; L79    lii
          L81    lii; L83 xxxiii
                        L85   xxix
Glynn, James            Scr  2:229
Glynn, James M.         Scr  2:232

Goble, Albert William
                         N70    528
Godbe, William S.        Goo    336
                         Ske    367
Godbey, Thomas L.        L61 Alpha
Godbey, Thomas M.        L63 Alpha
                         N70    336
Godbey, Tom              L55     67
                         L57 Alpha
Godecke, Henry H.        N70    925
Goicoa, Nick             Lam    244
Goicoa, Ramon N.         N70    630
Goicoechea, Elias Fernando
                         N70    417
Goicoechea, Julian       N70   1039
Goicoechea, Pedro        Sil    321
Gojack, Mary L.          L73 xxxiv
          L75 xxviii; L77   xxvi
Golden, Frank            Dav   1155
Golding, H.F.            Cur     69
Goldsworthy, W.E.        Bru     19
Gomes, Nancy A.          L77     xl
Gondra, Ernest           N70    880
Gooch, Mathew            Lam    245
Good, Joe                Lam    245
Goodale, Samuel W.       Dav   1156
Goodding, Leslie Newton
                         Rei     81
Goodfriend, Jacob        Dav   1156
Goodin, James T.         Dav   1156
Gooding, Jacob           Wre    650
Goodman, Dale            L77     xl
Goodman, J. Henry        Scr  3:480
Goodman, John Henry      Dav   1157
Goodman, William C.      Dav   1201
                         Scr   2:75
Goodman, William Charles
                         N70    348
Goodwin, C.C.            Ang    321
                         Jud     (2)
Goodwin, Harland K.      Mea    125
Goodwin, Millard T.      Dav   1203
Gordon, Algernon Wilbur
                         Suc    120
Gordon, Gurney           D07   (34)
Gordon, Lou              Bru     20
Gordon, Louis D.         D07   (32)
          Scr  2:420; Ske    267
Gordon, Louis Dahlgrew
                         M50  144-E
Gorham, George C.        Goo    107
Gorham, Harry M.         Wre    335
Gorman, Charles H.       W49    304
Gorman, Harold S.        Mid    161
Gorman, Thomas K.        Scr   2:46
Gorman, Rev. Thomas K.
                         Gor     33
Gorman, Thomas Kiely, Rev.
                         W49    304
Gosse, H.J.              Dav   1203
                         Wre    546
Gosse, Henry Joseph      N24    120

29

Gosse, Mrs. Josephine M.
           Cur    30
Gott, Raymond A.     Lab    17
           O'B   100
Gould, Warren H.    Scr 3:128
Govan, R.B. "Bob"   D15  (21)
Govan, Robert B.    Dav 1204
Grace, Frank M.     Dav 1204
Grace, Rev. Thomas   Gor    25
Graglia, John       Scr 3:478
Graglia, Joseph     Scr 3:479
Gragson, Oran K.    Cro    64
Graham, Bodie      Bru    15
Graham, Denis D.    Phi    39
Graham, Emma Elizabeth Graham
           Geu   244
Graham, Jimmy      Bru    15
Graham, Katherine Nevada
           Geu   248
Graham, Kathrine Haley
           Geu    90
Graham, Patsy      Bru    15
Graham, William B.  Dav 1205
Graham, William Boggs
           D07  (35)
Grant, Archie      Scr 3:428
Grant, Archie C.    M50    86
           W49   304
Grant, George     Lam   245
Grant, Henry Martin  Ang   397
Grant, John    Ang Facing 93
Grant, Sade J.     W49   304
Graunke, Emery W.   W49   305
Graunke, William   Dav 1205
           W49   304
Graunke, William K.  N70   835
Gravelle, Harry C.  Scr 3:233
Graves, Madison Bayles
           W49   305
Gray Brothers     Lam   245
Gray, Enoch       Wre   745
Gray, Harry       W31    27
Gray, John M.     Scr 3:61
Gray, Leslie B.    L47 Alpha
Gray, R. Guild     Cro    66
    L63 Alpha; W49   305
Gray, W. Howard    Scr 3:210
Gray, William Albert Dav 1206
Gray, William B.   Scr 3:157
Grayson, George W.  Elk   332
Greathouse, W.G.   Lab   105
           M32    47
Green, Charles     Moh    21
Green, Charles F.   Scr 3:285
Green, Earl       Lam   245
Green, Edward     Lam   245
Green, George S.    Scr 2:24
Green, George Sumner Dav 1196
       O'B  100; Wre   454
Green, James J.    M78    57
Green, Jonathan H.  Scr 3:383

Green, Jonathan Herrington
           N70   304
Green, Josiah Elton  W49   305
Green, Madge W.    N70   805
Greenberg, Charles  Lam   245
Greene, Edward Lee  Rei    67
Greenfield, George H.
       Dav 1198; Lam   246
Greenhalgh, John E.N.
           Scr 3:344
Greenhood, Otto    Moh    69
Greenspun, H.M. "Hank"
           Cro    68
Greenwood, George A. Scr 2:480
Greer, Henry H.    Wre   705
Gregg, John Irvin   Chu     7
Grego, Mateo      Ete   142
Gregory, Bernice    Lam   246
Gregory, Ernest B.  W31    27
Gregory, Frank B.   Scr 2:250
           W49   305
Gregory, Frank Bell  W31    28
Gregory, James     Lam   246
Gregory, Milburn R.  W31    28
Gregovich, John    Dav 1197
           Ete    42
Greilich, Louis    Per    59
Gresh, Cyrus Edward  N70   348
Grey, Marvin Berdan  N24   116
Grey, O.H.        Ang   658
Gridley, Reuel Colt  Tay   112
Grier, Herbert E.   Cro    70
Griffin, Robert Stuart
           W49   306
Griffin, Thomas    Wre   562
Griffin, Watson E.  Wre   635
Griffith, Donald Marshall
           N70   491
Griffith, Edmond W. Scr 3:398
Griffith, Edmond William
           W31    28
Griffith, Joe      Lam   246
Griffith, Robert B.  Scr 3:399
Griffith, Robert Beach
           W49   306
Grigsby, Edward S.  Dav 1198
Grimes, C.T.      N10  (36)
Grimes, Charles T.  W07    80
Griswold, Al      Lam   246
Griswold, Chauncey W.
     Elk  331; Scr  2:4
Griswold, Chauncey Warner
           Lam   247
Griswold, Chauncy Warner
           Hal    33
Griswold, Eugene    Wre   595
Griswold, Gordon    W49   306
           Lam   247
Griswold, Irwin    Lam   247
Griswold, Isabel Short
           N70   846

Griswold, Lee Harbin N70   1030
Griswold, Morely I.   Chr    17
Griswold, Morley      M32    21
     N59    17; Scr 1:575, 2:3
     W31    28; W49   306
Griswold, Morley Isaac
                      Myl    99
Griswold, Nevada Hardesty
                      Geu   153
Griswold, Tom         Lam   247
Grock, Wilda Birdzell
                      N70   503
Groesbeck, P.E.       W31    29
Groo, Scott           D07   (33)
Grosch, E.A.          Scr 1:130
Grosch, H.B.          Scr 1:130
Grose, James          Dav  1199
Grosh, E.A.           Scr 1:130
Grosh, H.B.           Scr 1:130
Grosh, Hosea Ballou   Tay    33
Gross, Harvey         Bix    75
Grossetta, Martin     Ete   107
Grover, Charles Wesley
                      Lam   248
Grover, Charles William
     Lam    248; Wre   363
Groves, C.H.          Per   134
Grubbs, Leander R.    N24   118
Grundy, Thomas        Lam   248
Gubler, Albert Samuel
                      Whi   278
Gubler, George Henry  Whi   390
Gubler, Jacob J.      Whi   375
Gubler, Ralph         N70   366
Gubler, Raymond Jacob
                      Whi   380
Gubler, V. Gray       Cro    72
                      W49   307
Guckes, Lucille R.    Phi    39
Guercio, James        N70   510
Guerena, Benito       Lam   248
Gugnina, Nikola       Ete   110
Guild, Clark J.       Dav  1199
     M32    33; M50    54
     Scr  3:33; W31    29
Guild, Clark Joseph   W49   307
Guisti, Marshall      M50 144-J
Guisti, Virginia Boitano
                      Geu   110
Gulling, Amy J. Thompson
                      N70   917
Gulling, Amy Thompson
                      W49   307
Gulling, Charles      Dav  1148
                      N10   (32)
     Scr 2:180; Wre   404
Gulling, John         Scr 3:500
Gulling, Laurence A.  W31    29
Gulling, Laurence Archer
                      W49   307
Gulling, Margaret J. Scr 2:181

Gulling, Martin       Scr 2:179
                      Wre   350
Gunzendorfer, George  M32   125
     Scr 3:471; W31    29
Gussewelle, Frank W.  W49   307
Guthrie, J.W.         Wre   328


Haas, Wales Averill   Doc   109
Hadfield, Dale        Doc   153
Hadland, Kenneth      N70   284
Hafen, Bryan K.       L61 Alpha
                      L63 Alpha
Hafen, M. Kent (Tim)  L73  xxxv
                      N70   425
Hagar, Thomas Elisha  Moh    47
Hagen, Frank Jacob, Jr.
                      N24   121
Hager, Henry          Doc    96
Hagerman, James C.
             Ang Facing 213
Haggin, James B.      M78    34
Haight, Andrew L.     Dav  1149
     M15 (2:49); M32    67
     M50   128; Ros    57
     Scr   3:28; W49   308
Haight, Andrew Levi   O'B   101
Hail, James Arthur    N70   288
Haines, J.W.          Ang   383
Haines, James W.      Ban   288
Hale, Chester         Esm    19
Hale, Drusilla        Whi   606
Hale, Harold P.       O'B   100
Hale, Ira             Esm    19
Hale, (Tommy) Lee     W49   308
Hall, Charles J.      N70   577
Hall, Darrell         N70   202
Hall, Edward F., Jr.  M78    55
Hall, Edward M.       M88    36
Hall, Ernest F.       Dav  1150
Hall, H.O.            L47 Alpha
Hall, Helmer O.       W49   308
Hall, Henry O.        Dav  1150
Hall, James           N24   122
Hall, Job F.          Mea   126
Hall, Joseph W.       W49   308
Hall, Raymond Lewis   N70   973
Hall, Warren S.       Ang   413
Hall, Wesley W.       W49   309
Haller, Chistian      Scr 3:296
Haller, Joseph P.     W49   309
Halley, John S.       W49   309
Halley, John Sylvester
                      M50   112
Hallock, James F.
             Ang Facing 64
Hallock, James Fanning
                      Moh    13
Halstead, Edward D.   N70   370
Halverson, Mrs. Bertha
                      Cur    64

Ham, Artemus W.           Scr  3:180
                          W31    29
Ham, Artemus W., Jr.  W49    309
Ham, Artemus Wineman  W49    309
Ham, Jane F.          A82    34
        A83  148; A85  150
        L81  liii; L83  lxvii
             L85  lxiii
Hamer, Edward E.      Scr  2:327
Hamilton, Byron Wesley
                      N70    458
Hamilton, Cyrus       Wre    603
Hamilton, John        Lam    248
Hamilton, Richard R.  N70    986
Hammersmark, Orva     Per    136
Hammett, Benjamin Franklin
                      Suc    132
Hammond, Ada          Whi    265
Hammond, Charles Julian
                      W31    30
Hammond, Francis S.   N70    614
Hammond, John D.      Moh    63
Hammond, Prosper      N70    456
Hammond, Robert       N70    309
Hammond, W.           Lam    248
Hammonds, Oscar H.    Gil     8
Hampton, Arthur F.    N24    123
Hancock, Lucile K.    W49    309
Hancock, W.C.         W31    30
Hancock, William H.   Wre    613
Hand, Lee             Mur    97
Handley, Isaac T.     W31    30
Hank, Caleb           Hal    97
Hank, Caleb (C.R.)    Lam    248
Hankins, Erastus "Ras"
                      Lam    249
Hanks, Henry G.       M88    37
Hanlon, George J.     Dav   1150
Hanna, John Laughton  Moh    33
Hansen, Angus         W49    309
Hansen, H. Lee        W49    310
Hansen, Kenneth H.    Phi    40
Hansen, Mathias       Dav   1150
Hansen, Sophus Fredrick
                      Mea    126
Hansen, Walter C.     W49    310
Hanson, Andrew N.     N70    848
Hanson, Elbert Arnold
                      W49    310
Hanson, Nicholas M.   Scr  3:195
Hanson, Norman E.     L55    68
Hanson, Ulysses S.    Scr  3:196
Harbin, Guy S.        N70    617
Harden, Frank A.      W49    310
Harden, W.D.          Ang    633
Hardenbrook, R.M.     L53  Alpha
Hardesty, _____     Lam    249
Hardesty, Edward Piat
                      Wre    452
Hardesty, Manford I.  L55    68
Hardwick, James L.    Scr  3:339
Hardy, Arthur H.      N70    238

Hardy, Clark M.       N70    401
Hardy, Clark S.       W49    310
Hardy, Roy Aller      M50    28
Hardy, Roy M.         O'B    101
Hardy, Royce          Scr  3:87
Hardy, Stanley Laird  W49    311
Hark, George W.       M15 (1:101)
Hark, George Webster  Dav   1151
Harker, Maude Anna    W49    311
Harling, Jesse Kier   N24    124
Harlow, Josiah Clark  Moh    25
Harmer, Albert E.     Lam    249
Harmer, Frank         Lam    249
Harmon, A.K.P.  Ang  Facing 116
                      M88    31
Harmon, George        L55    68
        L59 Alpha; L60 Alpha
Harmon, Harley A.     Cro    74
        Dav  1151; Lab    95
                      Scr  3:27
Harmon, Harley E.     Cro    76
        L49 Alpha; W49    27
Harmon, Harley L.     L75   xliv
        L77  xli; L79   lii
Harmon, James         Lam    250
Harnar, Curtis Sequoyah
    "Bill"            N70    841
Harney, Phil          Hal    121
                      Lam    250
Harpending, Linlay    Dav   1160
Harper, T. Clair      W49    311
Harper, T.H.          Scr  2:203
                      W49    311
Harper, William Chester
                      W49    311
Harrah, John          W49    312
Harrah, William Fisk  W49    312
Harriman, E.H.        Goo    342
Harriman, Edwin L.    N70    314
Harriman, Herbert E.  W49    312
Harrington, Arthur Henry
                      W49    312
Harris, Anna          Scr  3:448
Harris, C.N.          Jud    (3)
Harris, Charles N.
             Ang    Facing 341
Harris, E.B.   Ang   Facing 100
Harris, Gordon Barnes
                      W49    312
Harris, Harvey E.     N10   (94)
Harris, John E.       N70    986
Harris, Joseph C.     Dav   1162
Harris, Len           L63  Alpha
Harris, Thomas R.     Lam    250
Harris, Walter J.     N10   (148)
                      Scr   2:11
Harris, Walter James  Ros    34
                      W49    312
Harrison, Moses W.    Whi    313
Hart, Earle W.        M32    99
                      Scr  2:226
Hart, Fred.           Moh    64

32

Hart, Frederick Beckman
　　　　　　　　　　　O'B　101
Hart, James　　　　　Per　　27
Hart, James P.　　　　W49　313
Hart, Michael　　　　　N70　233
Hart, Thomas Clinton
　　　　M15 (2:73); O'B　101
Hart, W.H.H.　　　　　M88　　30
Hart, William J.　　　N70　847
Hartman. Arch E.　　　Scr 3:272
Hartoch, Kurt L.　　　W49　313
Hartson, David H.　　　O'B　101
Harvey, Charles C.　　M88　　28
Harwood, Cole L.　　　Dav　1161
　　　　　Jud (12); Scr 2:202
　　　　　　　　　　　W31　　30
Harwood, Cole Leslie　O'B　102
Hash, James L.　　　　Dav　1161
Hassell, John A.　　　D07　(38)
Hassey, Frank A.　　　M88　　32
Hatch, A.J.　　　　　　Moh　　14
Hatch, Andrew J.
　　　　　　　Ang　Facing 221
Hatch, M.D.　　　　　　Ang　561
Hatton, Charles　　　　Dav　1161
　　　　　　　　　　　O'B　102
Hatton, William D.　　Dav　1162
Hatton, William Davidson
　　　　M50　80; O'B　102
　　　　　　　　　　　W49　313
Hatton, William James
　　　　　　　　　　　W49　313
Haugner, Oley O.　　　Dav　1163
Haven, A.W.　　　　　　M88　　35
Haviland, Carlton E.　Dav　1163
Haviland, H.E.　　　　L49 Alpha
Haviland, Harold E.　　W49　　27
Haviland, Harold Earl
　　　　　　　　　　　W31　　30
Hawcroft, Lee　　　　　Scr 3:117
Hawcroft, Ralph B.　　Scr 3:116
Hawes, George　　　　　L51 Alpha
　　　　　　　　　　　L53 Alpha
Hawkin, Ernest H.　　　W49　314
Hawkins, Daniel Robert
　　　　　　　　　　　Dav　1167
Hawkins, Douglas　　　L51 Alpha
Hawkins, Douglas Morgan
　　　　　　　　　　　W49　314
Hawkins, Ernest H.　　Dav　1167
Hawkins, Harry L.　　　W49　314
Hawkins, John C.　　　Phi　　40
Hawkins, Leslie O.　　O'B　102
Hawkins, Leslie Oliver
　　　　W31　30; W49　314
Hawkins, Prince A.　　M32　　43
　　　　O'B　102; Scr 2:30
Hawkins, Prince Albert
　　　　　　　　M15 (2:27)
Hawkins, Prince Archer
　　　　　　　　　　　W49　315
Hawkins, Robert Z.　　Scr 2:31

Hawkins, Robert Ziemer
　　　　M50　72; W49　315
Hawkins, W.E.　　　　　D15　(31)
Hawkins, William E.　　Dav　1185
　　　　　　　　　　　Scr 3:413
Hawley, Thomas P.
　　　　　　　Ang　Facing 333
　　　　Moh　10; O'B　　35
Hawley, Thomas Porter
　　　　　　　　　　　Wre　398
Hawthorne, William A.
　　　　　　　　　　　Wre　709
Hay, Phyllis R.　　　　N70　570
Hay, Robert M.　　　　N70　543
Haydon, Thomas E.　　　Dav　1185
　　　　　　　　　　　Wre　646
Hayes, Karen W.　　　　A82　　36
　　　　L75　xliv; L77　xli
　　　　L79　liii; L81　liv
Hayes, Keith C.　　　　L73　xxxv
Hays, Granville H.　　D07　(36)
Hayward, Alvinza　　　Goo　202
Hayward, Horace L.　　W49　315
Hayward, Joel　　　　　Lam　250
Hazard, H.E.　　　　　L47 Alpha
Hazen, C.W. "Jim"　　　N70　488
Hazlett, Fannie Gore　Geu　　20
Hazlett, Mrs. Fanny G.
　　　　　　　　　　　Bin　140
Hazlett, John Clark　Ros　　23
Headley, Frank Burdette
　　　　　　　　　　　Rei　113
Headlund, John Alfred
　　　　　　　　　　　Ske　177
Heaney, Robert E.　　　L75　xlv
Heaps, William Henry　Mea　127
Heard, Lomie Gray　　　Geu　284
Hearst, George　　　　M88　　25
Heath, Constance L.　　N70　633
Heath, Richard W.　　　M88　　30
Hecht, Chic　　　　　　L73 xviii
Heckethorn, D.W.　　　N70　328
Heckethorn, Gene D.　　N70　328
Heer, A.A.　　　　　　O'B　103
Heers, Carol D.　　　　Cro　　78
Heers, Charles M.　　　Cro　　80
Heffernan, William F.
　　　　　　　　M15 (1:71)
Heflin, Charles William
　　　　　　　　　　　N24　126
Heguy, Alex　　　　　　N70　390
Heidenreich, Henry　　Scr 3:351
　　　　　Was　108; Wre　475
Heidtman, H.C.　　　　Scr 3:118
　　　　　　　　　　　W31　　31
Heidtman, Harry C.　　M32　133
Heiligers, Joseph　　　N70　388
Heimsoth, Dietrich　　Dav　1186
Heintz, Amy D.　　　　Phi　　40
Heintz, Donald J.　　　Phi　　41
Heise, Frederick　　　Dav　1186
Heise, Fritz　　　　　N70　896

Heitman, Dennis Otto N70    448
Helberg, August W.H.  Dav  1187
Heller, Amos Arthur  Rei    83
Heller, Maude Ellen Bonham
                      N70    816
Hellman, Herman W.   Suc    131
Hellwinkle, Elmer D.  N70    917
Hellwinkle, Henry    Dav   1187
Helth, Ed            Lam    252
Helth, John Wesley   N70    406
Helth, Ralph         Lam    252
Hemingway, William J.
                      W49    315
Hemme, August        M78     68
Hendel, Charles A.   L51 Alpha
          L53 Alpha; L55     69
                      L57 Alpha
Henderson, A.S.      O'B    103
Henderson, Albert S. Scr  2:69
Henderson, Albert Scott
                      W49    315
Henderson, Charles B.
          D15   (25); M15 (1:55)
                      Scr 1:510
Henderson, Charles Belknap
                      Dav   1080
Henderson, George S. Wre    748
Henderson, James R.  W49    316
Henderson, Leland    W49    316
Henderson, Margaret A.
                      W49    316
Henderson, Sally     Whi    557
Henderson, V.M.      Scr  2:324
Henderson, Virgil Monroe
                      Ros     55
Hendrick, Archer W.  M15 (1:67)
Hendrickson, Thomas  Chu     7
Hendrix, Edmund A.   Whi    407
Hendrix, Edmund Allen
                      Whi 319, 322
Hendrix, Ervin Lester
                      Whi 274, 397
Hendrix, Lucy        Whi    294
Hendrix, William     Whi    408
Henley, Benjamin John
                      O'B    104
Henley, W.J.         O'B     82
                     Wre    462
Hennen, George, Sr.  Lam    250
Hennen, George W.    N70    856
Hennen, Joseph, Jr.  Lam    251
Hennen, Joseph, Sr.  Lam    251
Henning, George      Wre    573
Henningsen, Carsten M.
          Dav  1187; Scr 3:422
Henrichs, James Rutherford
                      Rei    121
Henrichs, R.B.       M15 (1:99)
Henrichs, Rutherford B.
                      N10    (72)
Henrie, Christena Schow
                      Mea    134

Henrie, Gedske Schow Mea    135
Henrie, James        Mea    128
Henrie, Myra Mayall  Mea    132
Henrie, Parley Stewart
                      N70    221
Henrie, Rhoana Hatch Mea    133
Henriod, Gustave     N70    329
Henriod, Lawrence Doil
                      N70    329
Henry, Patrick       Dav   1222
Hepworth, Robert E.  N70    196
Herbold, Adam        Ang    409
Herd, Hugh P.        W49    316
Herderson, Charles Belknap
                      Chr     17
Herman, T.G.         Ang    646
Herman, Thomas G.    Wre    591
Hermansen, Christian, Jr.
                      Whi    596
Hermansen, Christian, Sr.
                      Whi    585
Hermansen, David L.  N70    573
Hernleben, C         Ang    410
Hernstadt, William H.
          A82   109; A83     56
          L77 xxvi; L79     xxx
          L81 xxxiii; L83 xxxiv
Herr, Helen          L57 Alpha
          L59 Alpha; L61 Alpha
          L63 Alpha; L73    xix
                      L75 xxviii
Herre, Albert William
     Christian Theodore
                      Rei     85
Herrera, Ciriaco P.  N70    633
Herrera, Edward      Scr  3:317
Herrod, L.F.         Per    134
Hersey, Milton James, Rev.
                      W49    316
Herz, Carl Otto      W31     31
Herz, Carol O.       Scr  2:221
Herz, Frederick O.   M50     64
          Scr 2:223; W31     31
                      W49    317
Herz, Richard        Scr  2:222
Herz, Rudolph R.     W31     31
Hess, James W.       N70    443
Hess, Joe            Lam    253
Hess, Marshall       Lam    252
Hess, Robert         Lam    253
Hess, William        Lam    253
Hesse, John F.       Scr  3:178
Hesson, Abraham W.   Lam    253
                     Wre    366
Hester, George H.    Wre    652
Hett, Paul M.        N70    515
Heusser, C.W.        Scr  2:436
Heward, Harlan       Scr  2:383
Heward, Harlan L.    M32     95
          M50   104; W31     31
Heward, Harlan Lester
                      W49    317

Hollingsworth, Paul M.
                  Phi    41
Hollister, F. Graham N70   911
Hollister, Stanley   N70   871
Holloway, _____      Lam   248
Holman, Harry W.     N70   201
Holmes, Alfred W.     Dav  1108
                  Ros    44
Holmes, Alfred Warren
              M15 (2:67)
Holmes, Alsop J.      M78    41
Holmes, Dewey P.     W31    32
Holmes, E.B.        M88    35
Holmes, Harold H.    W49   320
Holmgren, Arthur H.  Rei   139
Holmquist, Walter S. Dav  1219
Holmshaw, Harry F.   M32    73
Holmstrom, John      Per    78
Holst, Wallace L., Jr.
              W49   320
Holyoak, Sarah Jane  Whi   370
Homer, Kenneth      Lam   255
Honeyman, F.       Ang   387
Honeyman, Frank     Wre   541
Hood, Arthur J.     W49   320
Hood, Arthur James   Doc    89
Hood, Bert L.       Dav  1220
                 O'B   104
Hood, Charles       Doc    82
Hood, Charles J.    Wre   449
Hood, Elizabeth C.   W49   320
Hood, Thomas Knight  Doc   157
Hood, William H.    Scr 2:141
Hook, Jacob        Dav  1220
Hooper, Frank       Hal    79
                 Lam   255
Hooper, W.J.        Wre   324
Hooper, William J.   Scr 2:438
                 W31    32
Hopkins, George W.   Ros     3
Hopper, William W.   M50    24
                 Mid   135
Hoppin, John H.     Ban   263
Horden, John W.     Scr 2:457
Horgan, John E.     Scr 2:227
                 W49   321
Horgan, William Joseph
              N24   130
Horgan, William P.   W49   321
Horlacher, Fred     L49 Alpha
                 L51 Alpha
Horlacher, Fred C. W49 21, 321
Horlacher, Harry    W49   321
Horn, Nicholas J.   A82    40
      L77  xlii; L79   lv
                 L81   lvi
Horn, Nicholas J. (Nick)
      A83   74; A85   76
      L83 xxxvi; L85  xxxi
Horn, Paul E.       Cro    82
Horne, Charles      A85   111
                 L85  lxiv

Horning, William Keith
              W49   321
Horsey, Charles L.   Scr  2:63
Horsey, Charles Lee M15 (2:23)
        O'B  104; W49   322
Horsley, Agnes      Whi   580
Horsley, Agnes M.   Whi   375
Horsley, John Peckett, Jr.
              Whi   337
Horsley, John Peckett, Sr.
              Whi   336
Horton, Evaline E.   Whi   603
Horton, James       N24   132
Horton, Robert L.   Wre   552
Hose, L.M.         L55    69
                 L57 Alpha
Hoskins, Charles    Dav  1220
Hoskins, George S.   W49   322
Hough, J.P.         Lam   255
Houghton, Samuel G.  L53 Alpha
House, R. Bunyan    N70   468
Houssels, J.K., Jr.  L51 Alpha
Houssels, J. Kell   W49   322
Hoveck, Matt       W07   197
Howard, Benjamin F.  Scr 2:376
Howard, Edward H.   Phi    42
Howard, Mary Nell   Phi    42
Howard, Melvin      L61 Alpha
                 L63 Alpha
Howard, Melvin (Bode)
        L73 xxxvi; L75  xlvi
                 L77 xliii
Howard, Melvin B.   N70   618
Howard, Nick       Lam   255
Howard, William Davis
              W49   322
Howe, A.H.         D15   (23)
Howe, Albert Hovey  M15  (2:9)
Howe, H.H.         Moh    40
Howe, Hayward Howard Wre   496
Howell, Eugene      Haw     8
                 Wre   742
Howell, Eugene H.   Scr 2:289
Howell, John Thomas  Rei   123
Howell, William L.   Scr 2:228
Howland, Marta L.   W31    32
Howland, William H.  M78    47
Hoyt, Henry M.      O'B   104
Hubbard, _____     Lam   255
Hubbs, John Haviland Ros    20
Hudson, Less L.     N10 (112)
Huff, Darrell W.    L73 xxxvii
Huffaker, Dan      Wre   450
Huffaker, Mrs. Edith Taylor
              Cur    23
Huffaker, Granville W.
       Ang  628; Ban    86
Huffer, Frank E.    Scr 3:293
Hughes, Archie E.   N70  1046
Hughes, Howard A.   Chr    25
Hughes, Sylvan      N70   238
Hull, Cary          Lam   256

Hull, Elmer Everett     O'B    105
Hull, James Taylor      W49    322
Hull, Quincy W.         Dav   1221
Hulse, Benjamin Robison
                        Mea    141
Hulshizer, James Edwin
                        Suc    148
Humke, David E.         A83    178
        A85   180; L83 lxviii
                        L85    lxv
Humphrey, Charles A.    Dav   1221
Humphrey, Mrs. Frank Ellis
                        Bin    140
Humphrey, Frank G.      Dav   1221
Humphrey, Harvey R.     L60  Alpha
        L61 Alpha; L63 Alpha
                        N70    961
Humphrey, J.B. "Jake"
                        D15    (29)
Humphrey, Jacob B.      Dav   1223
Humphrey, John C.       Scr  3:406
Humphrey, John Carl     W07    232
Humphrey, Marvin B.     L47  Alpha
        L49 Alpha; L51 Alpha
        L57 Alpha; L59 Alpha
        L60 Alpha; W49     27
Hunewill Family         N70   1038
Hunewill, Harvey Eugene
                        N70    901
Hunewill, Stanley Hyde
                        N70    963
Hunken, Henry Christopher
                        Wre    536
Hunsucker, Alexander    N24    133
Hunt, Dinah Ann         Whi    361
Hunt, Leigh             Scr  3:110
Hunt, Martha Ann        Whi    324
Hunter, Douglas A.      Doc    164
Hunter, George          Lam    256
Hunter, Jack J.         L55     69
        L59 Alpha; L60 Alpha
Hunter, John            Elk    335
Hunter, John Handley    N70   1016
Hunter, John J.         W49    323
Hunter, Thomas          Dav   1223
        Lam   256; Wre    698
Huntington, Collis P.
                        Goo     65
Huntington, John        Mur    155
Huntington, Thomas Waterman
                        Doc     73
Huntsman, Clarence      N24    134
Huntsman, Don           N70    409
Hurley, Daniel J.       W49    323
Hurley, Denis           Scr  3:101
Huron, John E.          W49    323
Hursh, Ernest H.        W49    323
Hursh, Vern Victor      W49    324
Hurst, Nathan T.        W49    324
Hurst, Sadie Dotson     Ame    346
Hurt, William J.        N24    136
Husband, Bill           Lam    256

Huskey, H. Walter       O'B    105
Huskey, Harkey Walter
                        M15  (2:5)
Hussman, George G.      L47  Alpha
        M32   171; W31     32
Hussman, George J.      W49    324
Hussman, James Alden    N70    882
Hussman, Otto L.        N70    929
Hussman, William        Dav   1224
Hussman, William Henry
                        N70    990
Hutchings, William E.
                        Whi    401
Hutchinson, Joseph H.
                        D15    (27)
Hyde, Carl L.           W49    324
Hyde, Orson             Was    117
Hyden, Orlie M.         N70    264
Hyden, Victor M.        Phi     42
Hydenfeldt, Solomon     M78     33
Hylton, Florence        Lam    256
Hylton, John Jessie     Elk    337
Hylton, Lena Katherine
                        Geu     25
Hymers, Lewis           Scr  2:298
Hymers, Thomas K.       Scr  2:296
                        Wre    623
Hynes, Michael J.       Scr  3:218


Imelli, Samuel A.       Dav   1225
                        Scr  2:496
Immonen, Leimo Gabriel
                        Ros     83
Inch, Merrill J., Jr.
                        W49    324
Inchauspe, Paul         N70   1013
Inchauspe, Pauline      Gra    100
Inchausti, Andres       Sil    316
Ingalls, G.W.           Dav   1225
Ingalls, W.A.           Wre    476
Ingalls, William S.     Dav   1226
Ingersoll, Robert J.    L55     62
Ingham, W.H.            Wre    685
Ingram, Frank           W49    324
Ingram, Frank W.        Scr  3:374
                        W31     32
Irvin, Robert Grandy    W49    325
Irvine, Kit Carson      Dav   1188
Irvine, Martha F.       W49    325
Irvine, Thomas          Moh     50
Irwin, James E.         W49    325
Irwin, Stan             L55     70
Isaacs, Maurice         Gra     19
Isbell, C.V.            W49    325
Isbell, Mrs. Mabel C.
        L57 Alpha; L55     70
Ish, Marvin E.          D07    (39)
Ish, Milton C.          W07    179
Isola, J.A.             Wre    575
Isola, Louis G.         W49    325

| | | |
|---|---|---|
| Itcaina, Pedro | Sil | 318 |
| Itza, Damon | N70 | 569 |
| Ivers, Thomas | L53 | Alpha |
| | L55 | 70 |
| Ivins, Anthony Harold | | |
| | Whi | 275 |
| Ivins, William Howard | | |
| | Whi | 331 |
| | | |
| Jaca, Jess Joseph | N70 | 195 |
| Jaca, Juan | Sil | 414 |
| Jaca, Silvestre | Sil | 413 |
| Jackman, Eugene | Whi | 613 |
| Jackson, Albert S. | N70 | 574 |
| Jackson, Charles F. | Dav | 1188 |
| Jackson, John Wilbur, Jr. | | |
| | N24 | 137 |
| Jackson, Joseph Roland | | |
| | W49 | 325 |
| Jacobs, Mrs. Gussie | Bin | 140 |
| Jacobs, Lester Henry | N24 | 138 |
| Jacobs, Murial | Mur | 238 |
| Jacobs, S. | Wre | 572 |
| Jacobsen, Cecilia | Whi | 592 |
| Jacobsen, Harold J. | L47 | Alpha |
| Jacobsen, Harold J., IV | | |
| | W49 | 326 |
| Jacobsen, Lawrence E. | | |
| A82 111; | A83 | 100 |
| A85 102; | L63 | Alpha |
| L73 xxxvii; | L75 | xlvi |
| L77 xliii; | L79 | xxxi |
| L81 xxxiv; | L83 | xxxvii |
| | L85 | xxxii |
| Jacobsen, Lawrence M. | | |
| | N70 | 896 |
| Jaeger, Edmund Carroll | | |
| | Rei | 111 |
| Jaksick, S.S. | W49 | 326 |
| Jameison, James | Lam | 256 |
| Jamer, Gerthia | Gil | 12 |
| James, Albert | Scr | 3:164 |
| James, Clark | Dav | 1188 |
| James, Clement Laurel | | |
| | Dav | 1192 |
| James, I.E. | Ang | 587 |
| James, Thomas L. | Scr | 3:350 |
| James, Wallace V. "Walt" | | |
| | N70 | 544 |
| Jameson, Scott E. | Ros | 59 |
| Jamieson, Robert J. | W49 | 326 |
| Janin, Henry | M78 | 50 |
| Jaramillo, Abe | Cro | 84 |
| Jauregui, Mateo | Sil | 411 |
| Jauregui, Pedro | Sil | 312 |
| Jauregui, Pete | N70 | 573 |
| Jaureguy, Jean | W49 | 326 |
| Jeanney, Robert Louis | | |
| | N70 | 561 |

| | | |
|---|---|---|
| Jeffers, Art E. | Scr | 2:298 |
| | W31 | 32 |
| Jefferson, Ray L. | W49 | 326 |
| Jeffery, Emily Ann | Whi | 346 |
| Jeffrey, John E. (Jack) | | |
| A82 42; | A83 | 166 |
| A85 168; | L75 | xlvii |
| L77 xliv; | L79 | lvi |
| L81 lviii; | L83 | lxix |
| | L85 | lxvi |
| Jeffs, Lewis A. | D07 | (40) |
| Jenkins, Edith | Wre | 564 |
| Jenkins, R.D. | W31 | 32 |
| Jenkins, Thomas | Scr | 2:267 |
| Jenkins, W.T. | Elk | 339 |
| Jenkins, William T. | Wre | 564 |
| Jennings, William | Ban | 98 |
| | Was | 125 |
| Jensen, Andrew | Whi | 616 |
| Jensen, Anna | Whi | 384 |
| Jensen, Arendt | Dav | 1193 |
| Jensen, Caroline | Whi | 608 |
| Jensen, Christian Weaver | | |
| | Whi | 572 |
| Jensen, Hannah Aneena | | |
| | Whi | 337 |
| Jensen, James Hans | Whi | 583 |
| Jensen, John | N70 | 259 |
| Jensen, John A. | W49 | 326 |
| Jensen, Kenneth R. | N70 | 319 |
| Jensen, Niels Peter | Whi | 545 |
| Jeppson, Vern E. | N70 | 377 |
| Jeppson, Wayne O. | W49 | 327 |
| Jepsen, Earl F. | Scr | 2:170 |
| Jepsen, Hans C. | Scr | 2:169 |
| Jepsen, Hans R. | Scr | 2:171 |
| | W49 | 327 |
| Jepson, Dorothy M.C. | | |
| | Scr | 2:272 |
| Jepson, Earl Franklin | | |
| | N24 | 140 |
| Jepson, Hans Christian | | |
| | Dav | 1192 |
| Jepson, Hans R. | W31 | 33 |
| Jepson, Melvin E. | Cur | 36 |
| M32 77; | Scr | 2:271 |
| | W49 | 327 |
| Jepson, Oscar D. | L47 | Alpha |
| L55 70; | L59 | Alpha |
| | W49 | 327 |
| Jerrem, Jerry | W49 | 327 |
| Jessen, Frankie | Lam | 257 |
| Jessen, Neef | Lam | 257 |
| Jessen, Ray G. | Scr | 3:165 |
| Jewell, James Augustus | | |
| | N24 | 142 |
| Jewett, John, Jr. | Lam | 257 |
| Jewett, John, Sr. | Lam | 257 |
| Joerg, Charles W. | A83 | 220 |
| A85 222; | L83 | lxx |
| | L85 | lxxii |
| Johns, Orr | Lam | 258 |

Johnson, Albert J.     Dav  1194
Johnson, Antone "Tony"
                       N70   440
Johnson, Bob           Bru    39
Johnson, Charles Theodore
   "Ted"               N70   819
Johnson, Daryl Embert
                       N70   631
Johnson, Ernest M.     L63 Alpha
                       N70   825
Johnson, Ferdinand Max
                       W31    33
Johnson, G.S.          D07   (41)
Johnson, George S.     Dav  1194
Johnson, George W.F.   W49   327
Johnson, Gilbert Stanton
          Suc  113;    W07   160
Johnson, Gregory G.    N70   544
Johnson, Harry         N24   146
Johnson, Herman Carl   N70   978
Johnson, Hiram         Wre   625
Johnson, J.W. "Wes"    Wre   426
Johnson, James A.      L49 Alpha
          Scr 3:294;   W31    33
                       W49    27
Johnson, James Austin
                       W49   328
Johnson, James W., Jr.
                       W49   328
Johnson, Joaquin G.    Phi    43
Johnson, Kendrick      M32   147
Johnson, Kenneth F.    L47 Alpha
          L49 Alpha;   L51 Alpha
          L53 Alpha;   L55    59
          L57 Alpha;   W49    21
Johnson, Kenneth Frederick
          M50  120;    W49   328
Johnson, Lola Davis    N70   952
Johnson, Marsh         W49   328
                       M50   102
Johnson, Maybell Wood
                       N70   895
Johnson, Nels C.       Scr 3:335
Johnson, Norman        Mur   154
Johnson, Paul J.       W49   328
Johnson, Robb C.       Cro    86
Johnson, Thornton C.   W49   329
Johnson, Walter D.     W49   329
Johnson, Warren E.     L61 Alpha
Johnson, William       N70   812
Johnson, William S.    Dav  1194
Johnston, James        Wre   577
Johnston, Joe W.       N70   552
Johnston, Joseph W.    Scr 2:470
Johnstone, Roy J.      Cur    65
Jonasen, Gordon H.     Cur   118
Jones, Adell Hunter Case
                       Per   108
Jones, C.D.            Geo   280
Jones, Charles H.      N70   452
          Per  117;    W31    33

Jones, Cliff           L47 Alpha
          L49 Alpha;   L51 Alpha
          L53 Alpha;   W49    21
Jones, Clifford Aaron
                       W49   329
Jones, David R.        Ang   383
                       Dav  1193
Jones, Delmar M.       N70   550
Jones, Evan            Lam   258
Jones, Glen C.         W49   329
Jones, Glenn H.        L55    71
          L59 Alpha;   L60 Alpha
          L61 Alpha;   L63 Alpha
Jones, Henry J.        Lam   258
                       Wre   433
Jones, Herbert M.      Cro    88
Jones, Homer           N70  1052
Jones, J. Claude       W31    33
Jones, J.P.            M78    26
Jones, James B.        O'B   105
Jones, January         Scr 2:273
                       Suc   117
Jones, John E.         Chr    18
                       Ros    21
Jones, John Edward     Haw     4
          Myl   55;    N59     9
                       Scr 1:382
Jones, John Joseph     N24   147
Jones, John P.         Ang   591
          M88   24;    Pow   279
Jones, John Percival   Ban   149
          Chr   18;    Goo   283
                 .     Scr 1:288
Jones, John Sutphin    Suc   138
Jones, Joseph Ely      Wre   647
Jones, Lester C.       Scr 2:416
Jones, Lewis "Coke"    Lam   258
Jones, Marcus Eugene   Rei    53
Jones, Max Lamar       W49   329
Jones, Ray             N70   425
Jones, Raymond         Whi   607
Jones, Richard W., Jr.
                       Suc   150
Jones, Robert          Wre   391
Jones, Robert E.       W49   330
Jones, Robert F.       Scr 2:369
Jones, Thomas Jefferson
                       Mea   142
Jones, Thomas L.       W49   330
Jones, Tom             Lam   258
Jones, W.D.            Lab    18
                       Wre   644
Jones, William Dudley
                       O'B   105
Jones, Willis R.       Wre   735
Jordan, George L.      N24   150
Joseph, Charles        Bru     9
Joseph, Harry S.       D07   (43)
Joseph, Joe            Lab    47
Josephs, Joe           Wre   482
Jovanovich, Raphael    Ete   142
Juaristi, Vicente      Sil   315

42

Lemaire, Rene W.        L47 Alpha
                L49 Alpha; L51 Alpha
                L53 Alpha; L55    59
                L57 Alpha; L60 Alpha
                L61 Alpha; L63 Alpha
                           W49   339
Lemaire, Rene Watt         W49    21
Lemmon, Henry Albert
                M15 (2:11); Wre   443
Lemmon, John Gibbs     Rei    39
Lemon, Henry A.        W49   339
Lent, William          Goo    95
Lent, William M.       M78    30
Leonard, C.R.          O'B    35
Leonard, Harry M.      Dav  1093
Leonard, James M.      Dav  1093
                       M32    13
Leonard, M.A.          Per   135
Leonard, Norman Chester
                       N24   158
Leonard, O.R.          Ang   337
                       Moh     9
Leonard, Paul A.       W49   339
Lerg, Daniel L.        N70   973
Lerude, Leslie         L53 Alpha
Leslie, _____        Lam   262
Leslie, Alexander Fraser
                       N24   161
Leutzinger, E.C.       L55    59
                       L57 Alpha
Levisee, Rexford B.    N70   632
Levy, H.M.             M88    35
Levy, Herman           Wre   575
Lewers, Robert         Dav  1094
          Ros    35; Scr  3:22
Lewers, Ross           Was    73
                       Wre   551
Lewis, Arthur C.       Scr 3:303
Lewis, D.E.            Wre   332
Lewis, Donald E.       N70   352
Lewis, Frank R.        Wre   741
Lewis, James F.        Ang   569
                       O'B 32, 49
Lewis, John A.         Scr 3:129
                       Wre   466
Lewis, John F.         W49   339
Lewis, Warren Eldred   N70   891
Lewis, William Fisher, Rev.
                       W49   339
Lias, Robert           Cro   102
Lichens, Fred          Lam   262
Licking, Anna Pate     Geu   164
Liddle, Parker         N70   630
Lienau, Ronald C.      Phi    45
Lightfoot, Elvie N.    N70   585
Lightner, Joel F.      M88    32
Ligon, William B.      N10   (10)
Liles, Calvin J.       W49   339
Lillie, Chester Arthur
                       N24   162
Lillis, Henry M.       Dav  1094
Lilly, Benjamin J.     W31    36

Lind, H.B.             W07   150
Linday, James L.       W07   172
Lindsay, Frank R.      W49   340
Lindsay, Howard Wade   W49   340
Lindsay, J.B.          W07   210
Lindsay, James L.      D07   (47)
Lindsay, Sam F.        W07   208
Lindsay, Thomas        Cur    77
                       Ros    45
Lindsey, Joseph        Lam   262
Lindskog, Albert C.    Dav  1094
                       Scr 2:432
Lineup, Benjamin Franklin
                       Per     8
Linnecke, Harry F.     N70   641
Linnecke, Otto Albert
                       W49   340
Linscott, Jack B.      N70   641
Lippman, Etta          Cur    51
Lisle, Ralph Fairbanks
                       N70  1031
List, Frank W.         N70   654
Liston, Alfred P.      Scr 3:442
Liston, Alfred Perry   N24   163
Liston, Edward R.      Scr 3:441
Liston, William A.     Scr 3:440
Liston, William Albert
                       Mea   192
Litch, Andrew          Wre   425
Litster, George        Bru    24
Little, Patricia       A85   159
                       L85   1xx
Little, Thomas L.      W49   340
Littlefield, E.A.      Ang   294
Littlefield, Edgar Lyman
                       N70   516
Littleton, Ole Admundsen
                       N24   164
Littrell, Charles Franklin
                       Wre   701
Livingston, William D.
                       Ske   213
Lloyd, Ben T.          D07   (49)
Lloyd, George W.       Dav  1095
Lloyd, Richard B.      Dav  1095
Lockard, E. Keith      W49   340
Locke, Charles Robert
                       W49   341
Locke, Lee D.          N70   472
Locke, Madison Ernst   N70   255
Lockett, Roy T.        Dav  1095
Lockhart, James M.     O'B   108
                       Scr 3:317
Lockhart, Robert W.    N70   434
Lockhart, Thomas G.    W07   104
Lockhart, Thomas Gaskill
                       Ske   333
Lockwood, Chester Clinton
                       W49   341
Loder, Echo L.         Cur    34
                       Scr 2:312
Loder, John S.         N10  (152)

| | | |
|---|---|---|
| Loder, John W. | Scr | 2:312 |
| Loeffler, Linda R. | Phi | 45 |
| Loer, Carl M. | W49 | 341 |
| Loew, Harold Joseph | N70 | 360 |
| Loftus, A. Jack | Scr | 3:199 |
| Loftus, Andrew J. | Wre | 395 |
| Loftus, J.P. | D07 | (46) |
| Ske 337; | Suc | 123 |
| | W07 | 98 |
| Logan, Clarence | Dav | 1096 |
| Logan, Hugh R. | Wre | 522 |
| Logan, William F. | N70 | 926 |
| | W49 | 341 |
| Logar, Frank | Ros | 93 |
| Lohse, George | M50 | 144-M |
| | W49 | 341 |
| Lombardi, Louis E. | W49 | 342 |
| Lommori, Joe P. | W49 | 342 |
| Longabaugh, Sam | Was | 289 |
| Longabaugh, Seth W. | Scr | 2:125 |
| | W31 | 36 |
| Longchamps, Fred J., de | | |
| | M15 | (1:79) |
| Longchamps, Frederic J., de | | |
| | M50 | 56 |
| Longley, A.A. | Ang | 633 |
| Longley, Lester A. | W49 | 342 |
| Longley, Samuel | Ang | 433 |
| Lonkey, Oliver | Wre | 526 |
| Loomis, Anna F. | Scr | 2:307 |
| Loomis, E. Frandsen | L47 | Alpha |
| L49 Alpha; | W49 | 21 |
| Loomis, Eugene Frandsen | | |
| M50 144-L; | W49 | 342 |
| Loose, Herman | Dav | 1096 |
| Lord, Frederick C. | Wre | 583 |
| Lorrondo, Cecelio | Lam | 263 |
| Lorrondo, Faustino | Lam | 263 |
| Lostra, John M. | N70 | 197 |
| Lostra, Miguel | Sil | 317 |
| Lothrop, John | Ang | 501 |
| | Wre | 702 |
| Lothrop, Ruel | Scr | 3:126 |
| Lothrop, Ruel E. | W31 | 37 |
| Loveland, Orlin C. | W49 | 342 |
| Loveless, Edward E. | Phi | 46 |
| Lovelock, Forest B. | L51 | Alpha |
| L53 Alpha; | L55 | 60 |
| L57 Alpha; | W49 | 342 |
| Lovelock, George | Scr | 2:105 |
| | Wre | 336 |
| Lowe, James Everett | N24 | 166 |
| Lowman, Zelvin D. | L73 | xxxviii |
| L75 xlvii; | L77 | xliii |
| Lowry, Albert M. | N70 | 1004 |
| Lozano, J. | Dav | 1099 |
| Lozano, Joseph | M32 | 169 |
| Lucas, Anne C. | N70 | 1009 |
| Lucchesi, Aladino | N70 | 649 |
| Luce, Ben Daniel | M15 | (2:57) |
| Luce, Harvey Easton | W49 | 343 |
| Ludel, Leonard E. | N70 | 901 |

| | | |
|---|---|---|
| Ludwig, _____ | Lam | 263 |
| Lugea, Ramon | Lam | 263 |
| Luke, Charlotte Jane | Whi | 399 |
| Luke, Frank H. | Scr | 3:37 |
| Luke, George | N70 | 302 |
| Luke, W.J. | N10 | (26) |
| Luke, William J., Jr. | | |
| | Scr | 3:36 |
| Luke, William J., Sr. | | |
| | Scr | 3:34 |
| Lumpkin, Henry | Gil | 46 |
| Lundberg, Melvin E. | W49 | 343 |
| Lundergreen, Josephine K. | | |
| Scr 3:104; | W31 | 37 |
| Lundgren, Fred | N24 | 168 |
| Lundy, Albert Charles | | |
| | Dav | 1098 |
| Lundy, C.A. | N10 | (164) |
| Lunsford, Ed. F. | Lab | 26 |
| Lunsford, Edward F. | M15 | (1:75) |
| M32 145; | Scr | 2:26 |
| | W31 | 37 |
| Lunsford, Edward Francis | | |
| Jud (16); | O'B | 108 |
| | W49 | 343 |
| Lunsford, William S. | Scr | 2:287 |
| Luty, F.E. | M88 | 32 |
| Lyle, W.S. | M88 | 32 |
| Lynch, Charles | Gil | 6 |
| Lynch, Hannah | Whi | 281 |
| Lynch, Jeremiah | M88 | 39 |
| Lynch, William | Gil | 6 |
| Lynds, John Bunyon | Wre | 617 |
| Lyon, J. Paul | W49 | 343 |
| Lyon, John Paul | N70 | 520 |
| Lyon, Warren H. | W49 | 343 |
| Lyons, _____ | Lam | 263 |
| Lyons, Daniel | Moh | 25 |
| Lyons, George G. | Moh | 68 |
| Lyons, James S. | Dav | 1135 |
| | Scr | 3:193 |
| Lyons, Moses R. | Moh | 47 |
| Lytle, Mary V. Perkins | | |
| | N70 | 230 |
| Lytle, Mary Virginia Perkins | | |
| | W49 | 344 |
| Lytle, Roy E. | N70 | 330 |
| Lytton, E.B. (Ed) | Lam | 263 |
| Lytton, Edward B. | Scr | 2:424 |
| | | |
| | | |
| Maas, Edward E. | W49 | 344 |
| Macauley, Thomas William | | |
| | W49 | 344 |
| MacBride, James Francis | | |
| | Rei | 87 |
| MacCarthy, John D. | Doc | 164 |
| Macdonald, Irving | W07 | 76 |
| Macdonald, Malcolm | N10 | (54) |
| | W07 | 53 |

Macdonald, Malcolm L.
                          D07   (57)
Machacek, LaVerne D.  N70   1032
Mack, Charles Ernest
                          O'B   110
Mack, Charles W.          Dav   1219
Mack, Duane Emory         N70   836
Mack, Ernest              Dav   1222
Mack, Ernest Deal         W49   344
Mack, Maurice             Dav   1200
Mack, Oral Henry          O'B   110
Mackay, Clarence H.       Scr   3:9
Mackay, Dan               Lam   264
Mackay, John              Tay   157
Mackay, John W. Ang  Facing 56
          Ban   135; Chr   25
          Dav  1063; Goo   160
                          M88   23
MacKay, John W.           M78   21
                          Scr 1:278, 3:3
MacKenzie, A.E.           L47 Alpha
                          L49 Alpha
MacKenzie, "Burr" A.E.
                          W49   28
Mackenzie, D.             D07   (52)
Mackenzie, John M.        Ske   335
Mackey, Elizabeth Ann
                          Whi   347
Mackey, Will U.           Wre   453
Mackintosh, Richard       Goo   333
                          Ske   353
MacLean, Donald           Dav   1219
MacMaster, H.D.           W07   166
Macmillan, J.H.           D07   (58)
                          W07   113
Macmillan, Morris P.
                          M15 (1:129)
MacSherry, Harry J.   Scr 2:396
Madalena, Frank Martene
                          N24   170
Madarieta, Celso          Sil   317
Madarieta, Jose Maria
                          Bru   3
Madarieta, Juan           Sil   319
Madison, Charles      M15 (1:93)
Madsen, Albert            Whi   592
Madsen, Anna              Whi   623
Madsen, Edward Harold
                          W49   345
Maes, John L.             Phi   46
Maestretti, A.J.          Cur   14
                          W49   345
Maestretti, Antonio J.
                          O'B   111
Maestretti, Antonio Joseph
          Jud   (17); M50   50
Magarrell, William Melvin
                          N24   172
Magee, Dick               G85   5
Magee, George Richard
                          W31   37
Magee, Richard            Gra   63

Magee, Walter             Gra   62
Magnuson, Lucile          Geu   125
Magnuson, Martin T.       N70   406
Magnuson, Theresa         Geu   125
Magrett, Tessie           Geu   270
Maguire, Bassett          Rei   125
Maher, Alice C.           W49   345
Maher, Julia Carr         Phi   47
Mahnken, John Henry       Chu   7
Maine, Slim               Gra   21
Malley, Ed                Dav   1200
Mallon, Joseph B.         Ang   605
Malloy, Helene T.         W49   345
Malloy, M.W.              Scr 2:405
Malloy, Thomas C.         Wre   656
Malo, Philip A.           N24   174
Malone, Geroge W.         M32   25
          M50   34; Scr 2:322
                          W49   345
Malone, George Wilson
                          Chr   18
Malone, Mike              A82   46
          A83   112; A85   114
          L79   lvi; L81 lviii
          L83 lxxiii; L85 lxxii
Maloney, Paul Lawson Ros  74
Mancassola, Battesta N24  175
Mancebo, Frank R.         Per   30
Manente, Harry L.         W49   345
Mangum, LeRoy E.          N70   383
Mangum, LeRoy John        N70   382
Manhan, Albert Roger W49  345
Manhire, Bertha           W49   346
Manilla, George           Doc   160
Manix, Joseph Clarence
                          N70   268
Mann, A.L.                Bru   21
Mann, Curtis              W07   203
Mann, Kenneth L. "Pat"
                          Lam   264
Mann, Lloyd W.            L75 xlviii
          L77   xlv; L79   lvii
                          L81   lxii
Manning, Boyd B.          L61 Alpha
                          L63 Alpha
Manning, William T.       Arr   60
Mannix, Frank P.          W07   220
Mannon, Robert A.         N70   584
Manogue, Rev. Patrick
          Ang   207; Gor   20
Manson, Frank M.          D15   (39)
                          M15 (1:11)
Manson, Frank Marion M50  22
Manuel, Paul              W49   346
Mapes, Charles W.     Scr 2:122
Mapes, Charles Whitcraft, Jr.
          M50   62; W49   346
Mapes, George W.  M15 (1:103)
          Scr 2:119; W49   346
                          Wre   330
Mapes, Gloria M.          W49   346
Mapes, Irene Gladys  W49  346

McCrosky, Robert Earl  
                       N70    303  
McCuistion, Albert D.  
                       W49    351  
McCuistion, M.E.     L47 Alpha  
       L49 Alpha; L51 Alpha  
       L53 Alpha; W49    28  
McCuistion, Marion E.  
                       W49    351  
McCulloch, Hugh Gregory  
                       Ros     92  
McCullough, James B.   Wre   657  
McCurdy, William      Geo   297  
McDaniel, Clyde C.    W49   352  
McDaniel, Joseph B.   W49   352  
McDermit, Charles     Chu     7  
McDermott, Andrew J. Lam   267  
McDermott, B. "Bartholemew"  
                     Lam   267  
McDermott, Bart      Lam   267  
McDermott, E.U.      Lam   268  
McDermott, Frank     Lam   268  
McDermott, James     Lam   268  
McDermott, John T.    Lam   268  
McDermott, Oswold P. Lam   269  
McDermott, Pat       Lam   269  
McDermott, Patrick   Hal   120  
McDermott, Patrick H.  
                     Lam   269  
McDermott, Paul D.   Cro   104  
McDermott, Paul Donald  
                     W49   352  
McDermott, Thomas   Lam   269  
McDermott, William "Bill"  
                     Lam   269  
McDonald, Alex       Dav  1137  
McDonald, Angus N.   Scr 2:443  
McDonald, D.C.       D07   (55)  
                     Scr 2:440  
McDonald, Dan M.    Dav  1138  
McDonald, Daniel C.  Dav  1137  
McDonald, Donald J.  W49   352  
McDonald, Joseph E.  Ang   579  
McDonald, Joseph F.  M50    68  
                     W49   352  
McDonald, Lillie Pistole  
                     Cur   147  
McDonald, Marion Jasper  
                     M78    73  
McDonald, Mark L.    M78    36  
McDonald, Minnie M.  Cur   112  
McDonald, Oliver G.  Lam   269  
McDonald, Russell West  
                     W49   353  
McDonell, A.J.       Wre   559  
McDonnell, Frank    Scr 3:402  
McDonnell, Patrick J.  
                     Dav  1137  
McDowell, Samuel S.  Doc    82  
McElhiney, Albert L. Lam   269  
McElphone, Randall J.  
                     W49   353  

McElrath, Jean S.    N70   191  
McElrath, Mabell Lillian  
    Paddock        N70   876  
McElroy, Daniel     Dav  1148  
McElroy, Fred       Lam   269  
McElroy, J.F.       L51 Alpha  
       L55   72; L61 Alpha  
McErquiaga, Frank   N70   429  
McEwen, Arthur      Lew    29  
McEwen, Arthur B.   Ang   327  
                     Moh    62  
McFadden, C.J.      D15   (47)  
McFadden, Clarence J.  
                     W49   353  
McFadden, Clarence James  
                     O'B   109  
McGarry, Edward     Chu    10  
McGarry, Leonard B.  W07   214  
McGaughey, James W.  A85   141  
                     L85   lxxi  
McGhie, William M.   W49   353  
McGill, W.N.        Geo   310  
McGill, William N.   D15   (53)  
                     Dav  1152  
McGill, William Y.   N70   205  
McGiness, George    Bru    23  
McGinnis, A.F. "Mack"  
                     Lam   269  
McGinty, William G.  Dav  1152  
McGovern, Charles   Scr 2:492  
McGovern, Charles Morris  
                     Dav  1152  
McGowan, Dave Terrance  
                     N70   867  
McGowan, Wilson    L57 Alpha  
       L59 Alpha; L60 Alpha  
       L61 Alpha; L63 Alpha  
McGrann, Richard Philip  
                     Suc   156  
McGrath, John       Scr 2:127  
                     Wre   662  
McGrath, Philip J.   Wre   477  
McGregor, Thomas    Chu    10  
McGriff, Edwin G.    Scr 3:170  
McGuiness, George    G85     9  
McGuirk, Don        L47 Alpha  
       L49 Alpha; W49    21  
McInnis, Charles     W49   353  
McInnis, Guy A.      Scr 3:254  
McIntire, Alexander Dav  1153  
McIntosh, C.H.       Dav  1256  
                     O'B   109  
McIntosh, Charles H. D15   (37)  
                   M15 (1:47)  
McIntosh, J.A.       Per    31  
McIntosh, J.H.       Per    31  
McIntyre, Samuel    Elk   347  
            Hal   68; Lam   270  
McKane, John Y.     W07    88  
McKay, Dana        N70   246  
McKay, James        W31    38  
McKay, Mervin M.    N70   859

McKay, Walter William
　　　　　　　　　N70　1020
McKenney, DeWitt C.　Ros　10
McKenzie, George　D15　(45)
McKenzie, Joseph Charles
　　"Specs"　N70　632
McKenzie, L.E.　Lam　270
McKenzie, Roderick Due
　　　　　　　　　Whi　361
McKernan, Leslie　N70　1023
McKernan, Philip T.　Scr　2:409
McKim, Hiram Albert　Dav　1153
McKinley, Max　Lam　270
McKinney, John　Lam　271
McKinney, Lawrence E.
　　　　　　　　　W49　354
McKinney, Owen　Lam　271
McKinnon, T.O.　Scr　3:411
McKinty, James　Wre　631
McKissick, Howard B.　Dav　1154
McKissick, Howard F.　L57　Alpha
　　L59 Alpha; L60　Alpha
McKissick, Howard F., Jr.
　　　　　　　　　L61　Alpha
McKissick, Howard Frank
　　　　　　　　　N70　619
McKnight, Joseph Francis
　　　　　　　　　Lam　272
McKnight, William　Dav　1258
　　Jud　(18); M15　(2:53)
　　M32　57; M50　36
　　O'B　109; Scr　2:34
　　W31　38; W49　354
McLane, Joseph　Lam　272
McLaughlin, John T.　W49　354
McLaughlin, John Thomas
　　　　　　　　　M50　144-D
McLaughlin, Thomas J.
　　　　　　　　　W49　354
McLean, David　Dav　1154
　　　　　　　　　W31　38
McLeod, Angus　Ang　410
　　　　　　　　　Wre　580
McLeod, Charles A.　Dav　1218
McLeod, Charles Alexander
　　　　　　　　　N70　968
McLeod, Evan Wayne　W49　354
McMahon, Harry G.　W07　222
McMillan, William　Ros　16
McMullen, Hugh D.　L57　Alpha
　　L55　72; N70　614
McMullen, James H.　Lam　272
McMullen, Samuel　Wre　748
McMullin, S.G.　Suc　130
McNair, William F.　Scr　3:155
McNamara, Harry　Scr　3:408
McNamara, John　Hal　117
McNamara, John, Sr.　Lam　272
McNamara, John E.　W31　39
McNamara, John Edward
　　　　　　　　　O'B　110

McNamee, Charles David
　　　　　　　　　N24　187
McNamee, Frank　W49　355
McNamee, Frank, Jr.　Scr　3:183
　　　　　　　　　W31　39
McNamee, Frank R.　O'B　110
McNamee, Joseph W.　L63　Alpha
McNamee, Leo　N70　244
McNamee, Leo A.　O'B　110
　　　　　　　　　Scr　3:182
McNamee, Leo Aloysius
　　　W31　39; W49　355
McNeel, Richard K.　L73　xxxix
McNeely, Anna E.　Scr　3:20
McNeil, H.A.　Scr　3:83
McNett, Reuben Lyod　N70　649
McNew, Charles　Lam　273
McNew, John W.　Lam　273
McNew, Lee　Lam　273
McPhee, S.A.　Lam　273
McPherson, James　N70　485
McQueary, Howard Lewis
　　　　　　　　　N70　353
McRae, Duncan　Ang　562
M'Cullough, James L.　N10　(108)
McVey, Emerson K.　Doc　167
McVicar, C.A., Mrs.　Scr　3:327
McVicar, Neil William
　　　　　　　　　N70　905
McVicar, Roy W.　N70　855
Meacham, Robert S.　Dav　1228
　　　　　　　　　Wre　605
Means, Perry George　W49　355
Mears, Ardith V.　N70　365
Meder, B.H.　Moh　17
Meder, Ross　W07　236
Medin, Marco　Ete　32
Mehse, Louis A.　D07　(54)
Meigs, John Jerrold　Doc　60
Melarkey, David　Moh　48
Melich, Nick　Ete　130
Mello, Donald R.　A82　52
　　L73　xl; A83　82
　　A85　84; L75　xlix
　　L77　xlvi; L79　lx
　　L81　lxi; L83　xxxix
　　　　　　　　　L85　xxxiii
Melody, George　L51　Alpha
Menante, Ralph J.　W49　355
Menardi, John Blair　Suc　109
Menate, Frank L.　W49　355
Mencarini, Amos　N70　861
Mendes, W.F.　N10　(102)
Mendive, Esteban S.　Sil　322
Mendive, Prudencio　N70　414
Meneley, Charles C.
　　"Chuck", Jr.　N70　974
Meranda, Thomas Charles
　　　　　　　　　N70　520
Mercer, William Beton
　　　　　　　　　W31　39
Mercier, August J.　Dav　1228

```
Merialdo, Peter        M50  144-I      Miller, Ernest Robert
          W31    39; W49   356                            N70   456
Merialdo, Peter B.     N70  830        Miller, George         Per   134
Merkley, Ernest L.     N70  497        Miller, George Edwin   W49   357
Merlino, Laura Dell Hillyer            Miller, George J.      L47 Alpha
                       N70  430        Miller, Grant A.       Lab    28
Merney, Robert D.      N24  188        Miller, H.H. (Harry)   N10 (136)
Merrigan, Eugene Vincent               Miller, Hans           Lam   273
                       N24  189        Miller, Harold G.      W49   357
Merrill, Charles M.    W49  356        Miller, J.A.           Wre   500
Merrill, George Whitney                Miller, James Harold   N70   915
                       Ang  442        Miller, Joaquin        Goo   356
Merrill, Lillie        Scr  3:137      Miller, John Harvey    M15 (2:17)
Merritt, Nathan L., Jr.                                       Wre   420
                       N70  1048       Miller, John R.        Phi    48
Mesick, R.S.           Goo  260        Miller, Joseph A.      N10 (154)
                       O'B   76                               Ros    28
Meskimmons, James R.   Dav  1256       Miller, Joseph S.      Scr 2:111
Mestretti, Tony        Bru   13        Miller, Laura Dickinson
Metcalf, Vernon        W49  356                              N70   860
Metzler, Irene Suttle                  Miller, Lee            Lam   273
          Williams     N70  493        Miller, Lewis E.       N70   440
Mexican Joe            Esm   15        Miller, M.A. (Dr.)     N10 (166)
Meyer, Philip          Dav  1254       Miller, Major H.       Dav  1259
Meyer-Kassel, Hans     N70  872        Miller, Major (M.H.)   Lam   273
Meyers, Arthur G.      Dav  1229       Miller, Myles Max      N24   194
Meyers, Chas. W.       D07  (53)       Miller, Robert John    W49   357
Meyers, George H.      W49  356        Miller, Theodore J.    N70   443
Michal, Edward A.      Scr  3:241      Miller, Thomas Woodnutt
Micheo, Joe M.         N70  887                              N70   650
Mighels, Harry         Goo  245        Miller, Walter McNab   Rei    57
Mighels, Henry R.                      Milliken, Frederick A.
    Ang  Facing 312; Ban   170                              Scr 3:449
         Moh  23, 63; Scr 1:109        Mills, Allen L.        N70   502
Mighels, Henry R. (Hal)                Mills, D.O.            M78    32
                       Scr  2:108                             M88    38
Mighels, Henry R., Sr.                 Mills, Darius Ogden    Goo    56
                       Scr  2:106      Mills, Frances Jane    Whi   336
Migues, Sidney J.      N24  190        Mills, Lester          W49   357
Mijuskovich, Krsto     N24  192        Mineer, F. Edgar       Scr 3:415
Mikulich, Frank S.     Cro  108        Miner, Fred L.         Dav  1260
Mikulich, Sebastian F.                 Miner, Richard S.      D15  (49)
          Cro  106; W49   356          Minister, Rob Roy      N70   978
Milatovich, Vincent    Ete   38        Minnis, J.J.W.         N10 (104)
Miles, Henry W.        Ros   40        Minoletti, Ernest John
                       Scr  3:89                             N24   195
Miles, Josiah F.       Dav  1257       Minoletti, Guilio      Scr 3:316
Miles, Josiah Frank    W31   39        Minor, Gerald S.       N70   576
Miles, Minnie          Geu  270        Minor, Ira William     N70   454
Milich, Andy           Per   48        M'Intosh, C.H.         N10 (168)
Milk, Orval E.         Cro  110        Miramon, Jacques       Dav  1098
Millard, Edward        Dav  1258       Mitchell, Corbet       N24   196
Miller, A. Grant       Dav  1259       Mitchell, George William
                       O'B  112                              W49   358
Miller, Alvin          N70  439        Mitchell, J.F.         Suc   103
Miller, C.H.           N10  (78)       Mitchell, James        Lam   274
Miller, E.R. (Boots)   W49  357        Mitty, Rev. John J.    Gor    30
Miller, E.R., Jr.      L47 Alpha       Mobley, Honnor Elaine
Miller, Earl Ray       W49  356                              W49   358
Miller, Edwin H.       N70  859        Moe, Kermit            W49   358
                       W49  357        Moffat, William        Dav  1235
Miller, Edwin W.       N70  821
```

Moffat, William H.    D15   (43)
          M15 (1:73); M32      7
                     Scr  2:140
Moffat, William Henry
          Elk   351; Lam   274
Moffatt, William Henry
          M50   12; W49   358
Molenbeck, Cornelius N24   198
Molini, John Alexander
                     W31    40
Mollart, George Edward
                     N24   199
Moller, Niels R.     N70   215
Moltzen, Thomas      W49   358
Molyneux, Bertha Mary
                     Whi   607
Monaghan, Gerard J.  L59 Alpha
                     L60 Alpha
Monnette, M.J.       D07   (51)
Monroe, Warren L.    L47 Alpha
          L59 Alpha; L60 Alpha
          L61 Alpha; L63 Alpha
          L73   xx; L75    xxx
Monroe, Warren L. "Snowy"
                     N70   463
Monroe, Warren Ludwig
                     W49   359
Montero, Ramon F.    N70   468
Montezuma, Carlos    Doc   128
Montgomery, Bertha   Cro   112
Montgomery, E.A.     Scr  3:51
                     W07   192
Montrose, George A.  Scr 2:502
Montrose, George Albert
          Ros    75; W49   359
Montrose, Owen E.    N70   507
Moody, Don A.        L75   xlix
                     L77  xlvii
Moody, Donald A.     N70   594
Mooney, William      Ang   620
Moore, Mrs. Anna Virginia
          Chatham    Bin   141
Moore, Cedric Glenn  N70   494
Moore, Charles Francis
                     W49   359
Moore, Clyde B.      W31    40
Moore, Edwin A.      Scr 2:199
Moore, Frederick Pettes
                     N24   200
Moore, George        Doc   164
                     Doc   167
Moore, Gertrude      W49   359
Moore, Henry Iven    O'B   112
Moore, J.B.          Ang   390
Moore, J.D.          Lab    71
Moore, James G.      W31    40
Moore, Jerry         Moh    71
Moore, Joseph F.     W49   359
Moore, M.B.          Lab    19
Moore, Milton B.     M15 (1:85)
          N10   (64); O'B   113
Moore, R. Julian     Cro   114

Moore, Robert Taylor W49   360
Moore, Roxie P.      N24   202
Moore, Theodore C.   W49   360
Moore, Tredwell      Chu    11
Moore, Tredwell Woodbridge
                     Chu    10
Moore, William John, Jr.
                     W49   360
Moorman, Clarence R. Scr 2:488
Mooser, Charles E.   Dav  1140
Moran, Thomas F.     Jud   (11)
          M15 (1:95); M32    29
                     O'B   113
Moran, W.T.          Wre   592
Moran, William J.    W07    78
Morehouse, Harry V. M15 (1:65)
Morehouse, Henry Vinson
                     O'B   114
Moren, Leslie        Lam   274
Moren, Leslie A.     Doc   116
Moreno, Frank C.     W31    40
Morgan, George A.    Ros    29
                     Wre   554
Morgan, Thomas G.    Ban   269
Morgan, William Harold
                     W49   360
Moriconi, Ralph      W49   360
Morizio, J.          M88    32
Morley, Amarillious  Whi   608
Morley, George       Whi   549
Morley, Neva         Whi   594
Morrell, Franklin Thomas
                     N70   259
Morrill, Enoch       Wre   633
Morris, Byron E.     Scr 2:240
                     W49   361
Morris, Eva          Whi   258
Morris, Fred         W31    41
Morris, Fresno "Sandy"
                     N70   602
Morris, James        Dav  1234
Morrison, A.         Moh    54
Morrison, Daniel     Scr 3:315
Morrison, Donald E.  N70   938
Morrison, George H.  Ban   316
Morrison, James Allen
                     Ros    96
Morrison, William John
                     N24   204
Morrow, Dave         Lam   274
Morrow, John M.      Wre   439
Morse, Harold M.     W49   361
Mortensen, Martin    Scr 3:206
Morton, Henry A.     W31    41
Morton, Wells        Suc   114
Morton, William W.   Dav  1235
Moseley, John Ohleyer
                     W49   361
Moses, Thomas        Ang   581
Mott, Gordon N.      Jud    (1)
Mott, Gordon Newell  Chr    19

52

Mott, Israel            Ban     72
Moulton, Olin Cates     W49    361
Mount, Keith L.         L53  Alpha
                        L55     72
Mount, Lloyd            L49  Alpha
Mount, Lloyd Fletcher
                        W49     28
Mountford, Ida M. Browder
                        Geu    250
Moura, Virginia Moreira
                        N70    452
Mowbray, John Code      Cro    116
Moyle, Edward J.        W49    361
Moyle, Stanley          N70    590
Mrvosh, Bill            N70    402
Mueller, John V.        Scr  2:205
Mueller, John Victor    W49    362
Muguerza, Joe           Lam    274
Muir, Carl F.           Cur     72
Muir, Jean              Cur     71
Mulcahy, Edwin C.       W31     41
Mulcahy, Howard C.      Scr  3:283
Mulcahy, Patrick H.     Scr  3:282
Muller, Charles William
                        Dav   1236
Muller, Mary Honora     N70   1031
Mullich, August         N70    281
Mulligan, Chicken Hawk
                        Esm     47
Mullin, Charles Thomas
                        M15  (2:95)
Mullin, John            Bru      7
Mullins, Charles T.     Dav   1236
Mullins, Mona McCrudden
                        N70    968
Mullins, William        Mea    214
Munk, Harry A.          L47  Alpha
        L49 Alpha; L51  Alpha
        L53 Alpha; L55     60
                        W49     22
Munk, Jerry Lawrence    N70    596
Munk, Lester C.         N70    951
Munk, Robert L.         N70    563
Munson, Clarence Sylvester
                        Whi    560
Munson, Freda           Lam    275
Munson, John            Lam    275
Munz, Philip Alexander
                        Rei    119
Muran, Neal Lawrence    N70    642
Murdock, Charles R.     W07    152
Murdock, L.H.           W31     41
Murdock, Levi H.        W49    362
Murgotten, Francis Clark
                        W31     41
Murphey, Edith Van Allen
                        Rei    145
Murphy, Dan             Elk    353
        Hal     88; Lam    275
                        W07    218
Murphy, Donald A.       W49    362

Murphy, E.C., Jr.       L59  Alpha
        L60 Alpha; L61  Alpha
Murphy, E.C., Sr.       Hal    102
                        Lam    275
Murphy, Edward C.       Scr  3:376
Murphy, Edward Charles
                        Elk    359
Murphy, Edward Charles
    "Eddie"             N70    581
Murphy, Frank E.        Scr   2:40
Murphy, John            Lam    276
Murphy, John F.         N70    387
Murphy, John M.         W49    362
Murphy, M.A.            Moh     11
Murphy, Michael A.
    Ang  Facing 84; O'B 36, 52
            Ros    13; Scr   2:38
                        Wre    440
Murphy, Michael J.      Wre    673
Murphy, Milton Sharp    N70    815
Murphy, Pat             N70    819
Murphy, Patrick M.      L75      1
                        L77 xlviii
Murphy, T.C.            N10  (132)
Murphy, Walter          Lam    276
Murphy, William         Ang    369
Murray, George G.       Scr  3:145
Murray, John H.         L47  Alpha
        L49 Alpha; L51  Alpha
        L53 Alpha; L59  Alpha
        L55     72; W49     22
Murray, Thomas J.       O'B    115
Murrish, Harry J.       O'B    115
Musgrove, Mark W.       N10   (84)
Mushett, L.L.           W07     70
Mushett, Leo L.         Scr  2:403
Mussatti, David James
                        Phi     48
Myers, A.D.             W07    110
Myers, Charles          Lam    276
Myers, George T.        N70    464
Myers, George Tuohy     Ros     95
Myers, J.J.             W31     42
Myers, James E.         Lam    276
Myres, John W.          Phi     48
Myers, Marvin Albert    N70    509
Myers, Moroni           Mur     24
Myers, T. Gay           W49    362
Myers, William          Ang    390
Myles, George A.        W31     42
Myrup, Henry Joseph     Whi    555


Nagel, Ron              Phi     49
Nall, Richard Warren    N70    202
Nance, Carl B.          Scr  3:298
Nash, Richard           Wre    655
Naughton, Frank         W07    234

Norstrom, Glen C.       L47 Alpha
        L49 Alpha; W49     28
North, Al               D15   (51)
North, Edward G.        N24   208
Northrop, Stephen Abbott
                        Suc   132
Norton, Olive Stanton
                        N70   359
Nostrossa, Florentina
     Manuella Mesa      Geu     6
Noteware, Chauncey Norman
                        N09    48
Noteware, Warren Chauncey
                      M15 (2:81)
Novacovich, C.          Ete   131
Novacovich, John        Ete   142
Novakovich, Pero        Scr 3:524
Nowlin, T.W.            M88    32
Noyes, Charles G.       M78    51
Nungesser, Daisy M.     Scr 3:429
Nungesser, Earl W.      Scr 3:430
Nuti, Armando           N70   866
Nye, James W.           Goo   151
Nye, James Warren       Chr    19
        Myl   3; Scr 1:146


Oakes, Leon Jay         W31    43
Oakey, Reuben H.        Scr 3:330
Oat, Alfred             N70   346
Oat, John               N70   346
Oats, John              Scr 2:448
O'Brien, George L.F.    W49   364
O'Brien, J.P.           W07    66
O'Brien, James P.       Scr 2:161
O'Brien, James W.       Dav  1117
O'Brien, John P.        O'B   116
O'Brien, Joseph D.      Scr 3:160
O'Brien, Walter D.      D07   (61)
O'Brien, William J.     N10    (2)
O'Brien, William Shaney
                        M88    24
O'Callaghan, Donal Neil
                        Myl   135
O'Callaghan, Donald N.
     ("Mike")           Chr    19
Ocamica, Jose Andres    Bru     3
Ocamica, Maria Juana    Bru     3
O'Carroll, James        Lam   278
O'Connell, Ann          A85    64
                        L85   xxxv
O'Connell, Rev. Eugene
                        Gor    17
O'Connell, Mary O'Neill
                        W49   364
O'Connor, Charles       W49   364
O'Connor, Cornelius     M78    54
                        M88    25
O'Connor, Daniel W.     Wre   316
Oddie, T.L.             W07    51

Oddie, Tasker L.      M15 (1:31)
        Scr  3:37; W31    44
Oddie, Tasker Lowndes
        Chr    19; Dav  1066
        Myl    77; N59    13
        O'B   116; Scr 1:451
O'Dell, Edwin           Lam   278
Odermatt, Ernest J.     W49   365
Odiaga, Francisco       Sil   320
O'Donnell, Bertha       Whi   357
O'Donnell, Bill         A85   117
                        L85  lxxvi
O'Donnell, Charles Robert
                        Whi   370
O'Donnell, G. Loren     N70   205
Ogden, Peter Skeen      Ban    36
Ogden, Robert W.        W49   365
Ogee, Charles H.        L51 Alpha
Ogilvie, George B.      Lam   278
Ogilvie, George F.      Lam   279
                        W49   365
Ogilvie, George Francis
                        N70   564
Ogle, Pauline L.        N70   898
Oglesby, Melbourne Curtis
                        W49   365
O'Grady, James J.       Scr 3:192
O'Hara, Thomas Vincent
                        N24   211
O'Hare, Maggie          Geu   270
O'Hare, Margaret McNally
                        Geu   270
O'Kane, John            Wre   752
Olabarria, Pedro        Sil   315
Olaeta, Albert          L57 Alpha
Olano, Miguel           N70   450
Olave, Nash             Lam   279
Olave, Spain            Bru     3
Old Dick                Bru    29
Oldfield, Fred D.       Dav  1122
        Scr 3:424; W49   365
Oldfield, Joseph W.     Scr 2:433
Oldfield, Lyda          Geu   270
Oldham, Charles Francis
                        N24   212
Oldham, John            L53 Alpha
O'Leary, Daniel J.      Dav  1100
O'Leary, Francis Robert
                        W31    44
O'Leary, Jack Stowelle
                        Phi    50
Olinghouse, Henry I.    Scr 3:446
Olive, Chester O.       W07   252
Oliver, Charley M.      W49   366
Olivi, Harry            W49   366
Olmstead, Amos Cameron
                        Doc   123
Olmstead, William T.    Dav  1122
Olmsted, Amos C.        Scr  2:96
Olsen, Axel             N70   455
Olsen, Frank Emanuel    N24   214
Olsen, Olie             Bru    19

| | | | | | | |
|---|---|---|---|---|---|---|
| Parker, Amasa L. | Dav | 1124 | Patterson, Loyd S. | Scr | 3:527 |
| | Scr | 2:436 | Patterson, Webster | Lam | 281 |
| Parker, Amasa Lyman | Geo | 307 | | Wre | 388 |
| Parker, Chester James | | | Patton, James | Lam | 281 |
| | N70 | 498 | Patton, W.H. | Ang | 611 |
| Parker, E.L. | M88 | 28; 38 | Paul, Almarin B. | M78 | 42 |
| Parker, Fred F. | N70 | 591 | | M88 | 25 |
| Parker, George F. | Ang | 658 | Paul, Charles W. | W49 | 368 |
| Parker, Gilbert Everhard | | | Paul, Delbert Eugene | N70 | 517 |
| | W49 | 367 | Paxman, _____ | Lam | 282 |
| Parker, Robert Hazard | | | Payne, Frank M. | Dav | 1125 |
| | Ros | 60 | Payne, Harvey M. | Scr | 3:108 |
| Parker, William | Lam | 282 | Payne, T.L. | Lam | 282 |
| Parkinson, Ed. J. | Moh | 57 | Paynter, Harry | Per | 53 |
| Parkinson, R.R. | Ang | 315 | Payton, Donald G. | Phi | 51 |
| | Moh | 60 | Peacock, Carl R. | Scr | 2:371 |
| Parkinson, Webb H. | W07 | 144 | Peacock, Ed | N70 | 1032 |
| Parkison, Webb H. | D07 | (62) | Peacock, Oliver Cromwell | | |
| Parks, Bruce M. | L57 | Alpha | | Whi | 399 |
| | L59 Alpha; | L60 Alpha | Peacock, Oliver Merlin | | |
| | L61 Alpha; | L63 Alpha | | N24 | 219 |
| Parraguirre, Lorin D. | | | Pearce, Lester William | | |
| | L61 Alpha; | L63 Alpha | | N70 | 1014 |
| Parry, J.R. | Lab | 20 | Pearce, T.L. | Lam | 283 |
| Parry, Julius R. | Dav | 1124 | Pearce, W.L. | N70 | 489 |
| Parry, R.W. | N10 | (122) | Pearce, William | Wre | 628 |
| Parson, Mary | Gra | 100 | Pearl, Josie | Mur | 1 |
| Parsons, Edward Shier | | | Pearson, Ben | Lam | 283 |
| | W49 | 368 | Pearson, Melva W. | N70 | 500 |
| Parsons, Fred | Lam | 282 | Pearson, William A. | Scr | 3:74 |
| Parsons, Harry E. | W49 | 368 | Peavey, Carl O. | N70 | 295 |
| Parsons, Jewel Conner | | | Peavey, Webster Russell | | |
| | N70 | 429 | | N70 | 292 |
| Pasquale, Albert E. | L57 | Alpha | Peccole, William | W49 | 368 |
| | L59 Alpha; | L60 Alpha | Peck, Ferdinand W. | Suc | 137 |
| Pasquale, Alfonso B. | N70 | 460 | Peckham, Alfred R. | Scr | 2:44 |
| Pastorino, Thomas T. | W49 | 368 | Peckham, E.P. | M78 | 28 |
| Pate, D.A. | O'B | 117 | Peckham, George A. | Scr | 2:46 |
| Paterson, Andrew | Scr | 2:284 | Peckham, George E. | Scr | 2:42 |
| Paterson, Chester A. | Scr | 2:285 | | Wre | 414 |
| Paterson, William McKinley | | | Peckham, George Edward | | |
| | W49 | 368 | | Dav | 1070 |
| Patey, Henry | Wre | 624 | Peckham, James G. | M32 | 69 |
| Patocka, Frank | N24 | 218 | Scr | 2:41; W49 | 369 |
| Paton, George | Moh | 54 | Pedersen, John N. | W49 | 369 |
| Patrick, Edward Thomas | | | Pedrojetti, James Joseph | | |
| | O'B | 117 | | N70 | 573 |
| Patrick, Fannie B. | Scr | 2:365 | Pedroli, Malvin "Pete" | | |
| Patrick, Mrs. Fannie Brown | | | | N70 | 543 |
| | Bin | 141 | Pedroli, Stephen | Was | 143 |
| Patrick, Frank G. | Scr | 2:364 | | Wre | 471 |
| Patrick, L.L. | D07 | (60) | Peltier, Austin Lewis | | |
| | W07 | 124 | | N70 | 297 |
| Patrick, Samuel C. | Dav | 1124 | Peltier, Gary L. | Phi | 51 |
| Patten, Clarence H. | M32 | 163 | Pemberton, Elmer R. | W49 | 369 |
| | Scr | 2:292 | Penrose, Matt R. | Scr | 3:43 |
| Patterson, E.O. | Lab | 63 | Penrose, William R. | Scr | 3:44 |
| Patterson, Edward O. | Dav | 1125 | Peoples, Ronald L. | N70 | 214 |
| Patterson, John | Doc | 123 | Peoples, William T. | W31 | 45 |
| Patterson, John M. | Lam | 280 | Peraldo, Louis W. | W49 | 369 |
| Patterson, John Webster | | | Peraldo, Mario | N70 | 310 |
| | Lam | 281 | | | |

| | | | |
|---|---|---|---|
| Percy, Alexander O. | Ros | 30 | |
| | Scr | 2:235 | |
| Perez, Ed. | Gra | 59 | |
| Perkin, Hedley W. | Per | 135 | |
| Perkins, J.C. | L51 | Alpha | |
| Perkins, John F. | W49 | 369 | |
| Perkins, George | Lab | 23 | |
| Perkins, Reuben | Was | 83 | |
| Perkins, Ute Vorace | W49 | 369 | |
| Perkins, Woodruff | N24 | 220 | |
| Perley, D.W. | Moh | 49 | |
| Perondi, Alfred P. | W49 | 370 | |
| Perry, _____ | Lam | 283 | |
| Perry, Al | N70 | 502 | |

Perry, Charles C., Jr.
  A83  226; L83 lxxviii

| | | | |
|---|---|---|---|
| Perry, Donald | W49 | 370 | |
| Perry, Donald K. | N70 | 653 | |
| Perry, Harve L. | W49 | 370 | |

Perry, June Fulton Booth
                     N70   977

| | | | |
|---|---|---|---|
| Perry, Lizzie Ross | W49 | 370 | |
| Persson, Johannes | N24 | 224 | |
| Perumean, Pete, Jr. | N70 | 991 | |
| Peters, D.B. | Scr | 2:460 | |
| Peters, Donald G. | N70 | 543 | |
| Peters, Frank | N24 | 222 | |
| Peters, Herbert Z. | Dav | 1129 | |
| Peters, John | Lam | 283 | |
| Peters, John H. | N70 | 394 | |
| Peters, William B. | N70 | 484 | |

Petersen, Andres (Andrew)
                     Whi   623

Petersen, Christina
  (Johanne K.)      Whi   607

| | | | |
|---|---|---|---|
| Petersen, Lydia | Whi | 560 | |
| Petersen, Marius | Scr | 3:64 | |
| Petersen, Martin | Whi | 563 | |

Petersen, Neils Frederick
                     Rei   105

| | | | |
|---|---|---|---|
| Petersen, Peter H. | N24 | 225 | |
| Petersen, Soren | Whi | 607 | |

Petersen, Van Windous
                     N70   378

| | | | |
|---|---|---|---|
| Peterson, Edward C. | Scr | 3:88 | |

Peterson, Edward Charles
          Cur   22; Ros   50
                     W49   370

| | | | |
|---|---|---|---|
| Peterson, Lester B. | W49 | 370 | |
| Peterson, Louis | Lam | 283 | |
| Peterson, N.F. | Lam | 283 | |
| Peterson, Ray A. | W49 | 371 | |
| Petrini, Angelo D. | L61 | Alpha | |
| | L63 | Alpha | |

Pettis, William Eugene
                     W49   371

| | | | |
|---|---|---|---|
| Petty, Dee | Dav | 1129 | |
| Petway, Cecil Edward | W49 | 371 | |
| Pew, J.W.  M78  52; | M88 | 25 | |
| Pfeifer, Bill | Bru | 38 | |

Phalan, Frank A., Jr.
                     N70   480

| | | | |
|---|---|---|---|
| Pheby, Fred S. | D07 | (63) | |
| Pheby, Joe | D07 | (64) | |

Phelps, Arthur Thomas
                     Phi    51

Phillips, Alberta Perry
                     N70   809

Phillips, Alexander S.
                     Scr  3:321

| | | | |
|---|---|---|---|
| Phillips, Earl N. | N70 | 366 | |
| Phillips, Edward R. | Mea | 216 | |

Phillips, Frederick H.
                     Scr  2:224

| | | | |
|---|---|---|---|
| Phillips, Harry | Bru | 26, 29 | |
| Phillips, J. Warne | Wre | 689 | |
| Phillips, Jasper N. | Scr | 3:251 | |
| Phillips, Kate | Bru | 29 | |
| Phillips, Nathan | Lam | 283 | |
| Phillips, Pliny H. | Scr | 2:224 | |
| Phillips, Wayne L. | N70 | 463 | |
| Phillips, William N. | Dav | 1097 | |
| Piazza, Luigi Della | Wre | 616 | |
| Piazzo, Chester J. | W49 | 371 | |
| Piazzo, Lincoln E. | W49 | 372 | |
| Piccolo, Duilio | Lam | 283 | |
| Picetti, John | N70 | 806 | |
| Picotte, T.E. | Moh | 68 | |

Pickard, John Everett
                     Wre   334

Pickett, Samuel M.  M15  (1:43)
          M32  115; Scr  2:172

| | | | |
|---|---|---|---|
| Picott, T.E. | Ang | 308 | |
| Pierce, Doris E. | Phi | 52 | |
| Pierce, Keith A. | Phi | 52 | |

Piercy, Joseph Charles
                     Dav  1132

Piercy, Joseph Clifton
                     Dav  1132

Pierson, Clarence Grant
                     Dav  1131

| | | | |
|---|---|---|---|
| Pike, LeRoy | Scr | 2:135 | |
| Pike, Leroy F. | Lab | 17 | |
| Pike, LeRoy F. | M32 | 59 | |
| | O'B | 118; W31 | 45 |
| Pike, Miles N. | M32 | 135 | |
| | Scr | 2:22; W31 | 46 |
| Pike, Miles N. Jack" | N70 | 648 | |
| Pike, Miles Nelson | M50 | 52 | |
| | W49 | 372 | |
| Pike, W.H.A. | Ang | 371 | |
| | Jud | (9); O'B | 81 |
| | Wre | 506 | |
| Pike, Willard H.A. | Scr | 2:134 | |

Pike, Winfred Henry Asa
                     N24   226

| | | | |
|---|---|---|---|
| Pilkington, H. | N10 | (156) | |
| Pilkington, Harold | O'B | 118 | |
| Pine, Edward Leonard | Ros | 94 | |
| | W49 | 372 | |
| Pinjuv, John | N70 | 214 | |
| Pinson, Paul A. | Wre | 685 | |
| Pitman, Key | D15 | (59) | |
| Pitt, George Earl | N70 | 467 | |

58

Pitt, W.C.                W31    46
                          Wre   518
Pitt, William C.          Dl5   (61)
                          Scr  3:18
Pitt, William Charles
          Dav  1072; M15 (2:29)
Pittman, Edvina Jeppson
                          N70   861
Pittman, Frank K.         O'B   119
Pittman, Ida Brewington
                          W49   372
Pittman, Key              Chr    19
          Dav  1075; Scr  3:48
          W07    72; W31   46
Pittman, Vail             M50 144-G
Pittman, Vail M.          Chr    19
          N59    20; Scr  2:81
                          W49   372
Pittman, Vail Montgomery
                          Myl   111
Pixley, Myron             Lam   283
                          Wre   754
Plack, Ernest A.          N24   228
Plamenac, Mico            Ete   127
Plank, John               Lam   284
Platt, Joseph             Scr  2:99
Platt, Rebecca            Whi   305
Platt, Samuel             Dl5   (63)
          Dav  1098; Lab    59
          M15 (1:33); M32    31
          N10 (118); O'B   118
          Scr 2:100; W07   266
          W31    46; W49   372
                          Wre   708
Plaza, Emerito "Emmett"
                          Hal   123
Plaza, Emeterio           Lam   284
Plaza, Felix              Sil   316
Pletcher, Floyd R.        N70  1033
Plumb, Edmund             Scr  2:369
Plummer, John Ross        N70   395
Plunkett, Thomas C.       Lam   284
Pohl, Robert G.           Dav  1101
Pohlabel, Harry A.        W49   373
Poli, John, Jr.           N70   866
Polin, Henry              Dav  1102
Polish, John              A82    56
          L75     1; L77 xlviii
          L79   lxi; L81  lxii
Polk, Milt                Lam   284
Polkinghorne, Walter J.
                          N70   433
Pollard, Amos K.          Wre   740
Pollock, James            Dav  1102
Pomeroy, E.A.             Scr  2:482
Poole, Jeff D.            W31    46
Pooly, John H.            Wre   343
Porteous, Samuel G.       Dav  1138
Posin, Bernard            L61 Alpha
                          L63 Alpha
Post, Theodore H.         W49   373

Poston, William Kenneth, Jr.
                          Phi    52
Potts, Stanley            N70   502
Poujade, J.               O'B   119
Poulsen, Wayne            Bix   107
Poulson, Fred M.          Doc   109
Powell, Edmond J.         Scr  3:494
Powell, Harry F.          Scr  2:413
Powell, S.W.              Moh    51
Powell, Thomas E.         O'B   120
                          Scr  3:360
Powers, Mrs. M.A.         Scr  3:514
Powers, William F.        Cur   129
Powning, C.C.             Moh    16
                          Scr  3:81
Powning, Christopher
     Columbus             Ang   329
Powning, Joseph           M88    37
Pozzi, Archie             Scr  2:338
Pozzi, Archie, Jr.        L55    73
          L57 Alpha; L59 Alpha
          L60 Alpha; L61 Alpha
          L63 Alpha; L73   xxi
                          W49   373
Pozzi, Archie, Sr.        W49   373
Prater, Nicholas          Wre   716
Pratt, A.C.               Haw    16
Pratt, Bert               Lam   284
Pratt, Mrs. Emma Diehm
                          Bin   141
Pratt, Walter Elisha      Ros    46
Pray, Winfred A.          W31    47
Prediger, John            Lam   285
Prengaman, Paul           A82    58
          L79   lxi; L81  liii
Presti, Joseph Michael
                          W49   374
Preston, Fred A.          Per   126
Preston, R.M. "Bob"       Dl5   (65)
Preston, Robert M.        Scr  2:255
Price, George Frederic
                          Chu    12
Price, Jack L.            Scr  3:169
Price, Jennie Ellsworth
                          W49   374
Price, John L.            Scr  3:169
Price, Joseph Adelbert
                          Mea   218
Price, Robert E. (Bob)
          A82    60; A83   151
          A85   153; L75    li
          L77  xlix; L79 lxxii
          L81  lxiv; L83 lxxix
                    L85 lxxvii
Price, Robert M.          Scr  2:16
Price, W.C.               Moh    26
Price, W.R.               Chu    12
Price, William E.
                Was   123, 285
Priest, Alice M.          W31    47
Priest, Charles           Scr  2:321
Priest, D.W.              W31    47

| | | | |
|---|---|---|---|
| Raycraft, Joseph | Wre | 470 | |
| Raymond, Edward L. | W07 | 238 | |
| Read, Charles E. | N70 | 405 | |
| Read, John M. | Doc | 154 | |
| Read, John T. | M32 | 161 | |
| | Scr | 2:198 | |
| Read, Thonrton A. | Lab | 21 | |
| Read, Thornton A., Sr. | | | |
| | Scr | 2:197 | |
| Reborse, Lee George | N70 | 1033 | |
| Reboule, Charles | Lam | 286 | |
| Recanzone, Carlo A. | N70 | 430 | |
| Recanzone, Edmond B. | N70 | 972 | |
| | W49 | 377 | |
| Recatume, Domingo | Sil | 318 | |
| Record, Harry | Scr | 2:275 | |
| Records, Edward | W49 | 377 | |
| Redd, Della | Whi | 331 | |
| Redd, Farozine Ellen | Whi | 341 | |
| Reddy, Myrtle Irene Avanzino | | | |
| | N70 | 897 | |
| Redelius, Reinhold | W49 | 377 | |
| Redelsperger, Kenneth K. | | | |
| A82 | 64; A83 | 208 | |
| A85 | 96; L81 | lxvi | |
| L83 | lxxx; L85 | xxxviii | |
| Redman, Charles E. | Dav | 1229 | |
| Redman, Edward T. | W49 | 377 | |
| Redman, James Ralph | N70 | 567 | |
| Redman, Joseph R. | Dav | 1230 | |
| | Scr | 2:299 | |
| Reed, Earl D. | W49 | 377 | |
| Reed, Effie Jane Oxborrow | | | |
| Long | Geu | 275 | |
| Reed, Flo Z. | N70 | 833 | |
| Reed, Frank M. | W49 | 377 | |
| Reed, Henry M. | Lam | 286 | |
| Reed, Jacob Wheeler | N70 | 463 | |
| Reed, Lois | W49 | 377 | |
| Reedy, David | Dav | 1230 | |
| Rees, John T. | Doc | 131 | |
| Rees, Kenneth L. | Scr | 3:508 | |
| Reese, John | Ban | 69 | |
| Reese, Joseph B. | W31 | 48 | |
| Reeves, Charles R. | Dav | 1139 | |
| Reeves, Claude N. | N70 | 617 | |
| Regan, Edward | Dav | 1230 | |
| Regnier, Robert Roy | N70 | 610 | |
| Reid, Alexander Kirkwood | | | |
| | Whi | 347 | |
| Reid, Chester Flynn | N24 | 232 | |
| Reid, Gordon Mackey | Whi | 394 | |
| Reid, H.E. | Scr | 2:385 | |
| Reid, Harry | Arr | 63 | |
| Reid, Harry M. | L73 | xiii | |
| Reid, Hosea E. | Dav | 1231 | |
| Reid, Hugh Alexander | Whi | 265 | |
| Reid, John T. | Dav | 1232 | |
| Per | 63; Scr | 3:227 | |
| Reid, Lauren Gilbert | N24 | 234 | |
| Reid, Margaret | Whi | 397 | |
| Reid, Robert | Whi | 339 | |

| | | | |
|---|---|---|---|
| Reid, Robert James | Wre | 319 | |
| Reid, Walter G. | L51 | Alpha | |
| | L53 | Alpha | |
| Reid, Wilberta Grace | N70 | 397 | |
| Reik, Carl | Esm | 43 | |
| Reinhart, E. | Dav | 1232 | |
| Reinhart, Edgar | W31 | 48 | |
| Reinhart, Eli | Wre | 660 | |
| Reinhart, Moses | D15 | (67) | |
| Reinken, Charles | Lam | 286 | |
| Reinken, Fredrick | Hal | 80 | |
| Reinken, Fredrick J. | Lam | 286 | |
| Reinken, Hattie Drown | | | |
| | N70 | 618 | |
| Reischke, Herman | D07 | (72) | |
| Renfro, Lee | Lam | 287 | |
| Reno, Ellwood | Scr | 2:151 | |
| Reno, Elwood F. | W49 | 378 | |
| Renshaw, George T. | Scr | 2:412 | |
| Requa, Isaac Lawrence | | | |
| | Elk | 338 | |
| Reston, Zoe | Bru | 8 | |
| Restos, James P. (Demetrios | | | |
| P.) | N24 | 235 | |
| Revert, Albert L. | N70 | 323 | |
| Revert, Robert A. | L53 | Alpha | |
| L57 | Alpha; L59 | Alpha | |
| L60 | Alpha; L61 | Alpha | |
| Reymers, Bernhard H. | Ang | 411 | |
| Reymers, William A. | Wre | 755 | |
| Reynolds, C. Sumner | W31 | 48 | |
| Reynolds, Ray W. | N70 | 387 | |
| Reynolds, Rodney J. | L53 | Alpha | |
| | L55 | 73 | |
| Reynolds, Spencer | N10 | (186) | |
| Reynolds, W.R. | W31 | 48 | |
| Rhoads, Dean A. | A82 | 66 | |
| A85 | 99; L77 | xlviii | |
| L79 | lxiii; L81 | lxvi | |
| | L85 | xxxix | |
| Rhodes, Carlton E. | Scr | 2:214 | |
| Rhodes, Mrs. Iva Rowland | | | |
| | Cur | 102 | |
| Rhodes, J. Milton | Scr | 3:223 | |
| Rhodes, Jessie M. | Cur | 100 | |
| Ricci, Joseph J. | N70 | 805 | |
| Rice, Asoph | Mea | 219 | |
| Rice, Gordon W. | Jud | (22) | |
| | M50 | 132 | |
| Rice, James Randall | W49 | 378 | |
| Rice, Windsor V. | D07 | (67) | |
| | Ske | 169 | |
| Richard, Andrew J. | Scr | 3:492 | |
| Richard, Andy J. | W31 | 48 | |
| Richard, George W. | Dav | 1253 | |
| Richards, Charles A. | Scr | 2:7 | |
| | Wre | 665 | |
| Richards, Charles J. | Dav | 1233 | |
| Richards, Charles L. | M32 | 53 | |
| Scr | 1:535; | 2:5 | |
| | W31 | 48 | |

Richards, Charles Lenmore
    Chr   20; M50   82
Richards, H. Bramley  W49   378
Richards, J.W.      Ang   370
Richards, Maud      Scr 2:491
Richards, Robert    O'B   120
Richards, Walter B.  W49   378
Richards, Walter J.  W49   378
Richardson, Abner Stanton
               Ang   411
Richardson, Edna M. Boucher
               N70   822
Richardson, Eli N.   Scr 3:130
Richardson, Hannah   Whi   388
Richardson, Jack A.  W49   378
Richardson, Rodney Hall
               Dav  1234
Rickard, G.L. "Tex"  D07  (66)
Ricketts, Victor L. M15 (2:33)
Rickey, T.B.       W07   263
Rickey, Thomas B.   Wre   364
Riddell, Clara W.   N70   517
Riddell, Ruth L.    N70   517
Riddell, Samuel    Wre   527
Riddick, Bert Biggs  W49   379
Riddle, Alfred L.   W49   379
Riddle, Frank      Wre   482
Riddle, Howard     Wre   482
Ridge, W.R.       W07   271
Ridge, W. Roy     D07  (69)
Riding, George Kerry Mea   220
Riek, Carl S.     Scr 3:131
Riepe, Carrie      Geu   125
Riepe, Richard A.   D07  (71)
Riepe, Theresa     Geu   125
Rife, Leonard O.    N70  1004
Riggs, Al S.       D07  (70)
Riggs, Brigham E. "Slim"
               N70   930
Riggs, John Arthur   Phi    53
Rilea, Bernard A.   N70   445
Riley, Ella S.     Cur   130
Riley, Frank G.    W49   379
Riley, Harry A.    W49   379
Riley, Linford     L53 Alpha
Riley, Malachi M.   Scr 2:471
Riley, Mary O.     Scr 2:472
Riley, Zoe M.     W49   379
Rinckel, Mathias    Ang   561
Ring, Oris        N09    50
Ring, Orvis       Scr 1:434
      Was   272; Wre   524
Ringlee, Albert W.  W49   380
Riordan, James     Whi   285
Riordan, Jennie    Geu   270
Riordan, Maggie    Whi   285
Riordan, Michael Lawrence
               Whi   281
Rising, Richard    Ang   583
Risley, Mortimer Wayne
               W49   380

Riter, Henry       Dav  1244
      Scr 3:197; Was   249
               Wre   676
Rivers, Ira La, II   Rei   141
Rives, Henry      Ang   443
               Scr 2:166
Rives, Henry M.    M32    85
      Scr 2:165; W31    49
Rives, Henry Macon M15 (2:51)
               M50   108
Roach, Amos       Lam   287
Roach, William     Scr 2:495
Roantree, Robert Peter
               Doc   110
Robb, Daniel James   W31    49
Robbins, John E.    L47 Alpha
      L49 Alpha; L51 Alpha
      L53 Alpha; W49   23, 380
Robear, Newman    N70   196
Roberson, Amy L.    W49   380
Roberti, Gino      N24   236
Roberts, Alice Gluyas
               N70   921
Roberts, Benjamin Franklin
               N70   370
Roberts, Bill      Lam   287
Roberts, Billy J.   N70   313
Roberts, Dillon    Wre   534
Roberts, E.E.      O'B   120
               Scr  2:77
Roberts, Edward J.   Suc   121
Roberts, Edwin E.   W31    49
               M32     5
Roberts, Edwin Ewing Chr    20
               Scr 1:451
Roberts, Frank     Mur   113
Roberts, Garnett Kenneth
               N70   876
Roberts, Gary Lee    A85   156
               L85  lxxix
Roberts, George D.   M78    48
Roberts, Gerald A.   W49   380
Roberts, Paul D.    Dav  1253
Roberts, Sadie     Scr  2:79
Roberts, Thomas Edison
               N24   237
Roberts, Thomas L.   W49   380
Robertson, Glenn Lenore
    Taylor        Geu   263
Robertson, Joseph H.  Rei   157
Robins, Clifford E.  Dav  1254
               O'B   120
Robins, F.C.       Wre   672
Robins, Frank W.    L53 Alpha
Robins, Howard Vernon
               N24   238
Robinson, B.H.     Lam   287
Robinson, Douglas   Mur   256
Robinson, Florence B.
               Phi    54
Robinson, George    Ros     4
Robinson, J.A. "Pap" Lam   287

Robinson, J. LaRue      M32    41
                        Scr  2:147
Robinson, John Evans    W49    380
Robinson, Lester L.     M78    49
                        M88    33
Robinson, Robert E.     A82    68
        L73   xli; L75   1i
        L77     1; L79   lxiv
                        L81   lxvii
Robinson, Robert E. (Bob)
        A83    69; A85   71
        L83   xlii; L85   xl
Robinson, Sidney W.     W31    49
Robinson, Sidney William
        M50   100; W49   381
Robinson, Thomas        Moh    36
Robinson, Thomas S.     D07   (65)
                        Dav   1254
Robinson, Thomas William
                        W49    381
Robinson, Tod           Goo    100
        O'B    62; Shu   495
Robinson, W.K.          W07    120
Robison, Berton Henry
        Geo   335; N70   377
Robison, Doyle C.       Scr  2:437
Robison, George W.      Scr  3:214
Robison, Newal J.       W49    381
Robison, Roy L.         Cur    49
                        Dav   1175
Rochon, Joseph          Dav   1179
Rockwell, Bert          Lam    287
Rockwell, Leon H.       Scr  3:409
                        W31    49
Rodenbah, Jacob         Dav   1179
Roe, Herbert E.         W49    381
Roeder, John F.         W31    50
Roff, N.W.              Moh    72
Roff, Nate W.           Wre    714
Rogan, Marian Bell      N70    460
Rogers, Billy           Mur    18
Rogers, Edward H.       N70    842
Rogers, George Alfred
        M50   130; W49   381
Rogers, John Adams      Dav   1177
Rogers, Lewis H.        D07   (73)
Rogers, Thad W.         N70    525
Rogers, William Arthur
                        Dav   1178
Rohlfing, Harold J.     W49    382
Rolfe, Henry            Ang    584
                        Ros    14
Rollins, Garvice Charles
                        N70    454
Romeo, Albert           L61  Alpha
Rong, George W.         N70    954
Ronnow, Charles C.      Dav   1173
                        Scr  3:134
Ronnow, Christian Peter
                        Mea    221
Ronnow, Christian Peter, Jr.
                        Mea    225

Ronnow, Dan J.          W49    382
Ronnow, Daniel Jorgen
                        Mea    227
Ronnow, Emelia Laurine Hansen
                        Mea    221
Ronnow, James Price     W49    382
Ronnow, Joe S.          W49    382
Ronnow, Joseph          Mea    226
Ronnow, Mary Wardell    Mea    225
Ronzone, A.B.           Scr  3:510
Ronzone, Bertha         Cro    122
Ronzone, Bertha B.      W49    382
Ronzone, Bertha Bishop
                        Ame    349
Rooklidge, C.D.         D07   (68)
Rookstool, Wayne        N70   1020
Roop, Isaac Newton      Shu    405
Root, Ray               M50    110
Root, Ray J.            W49    383
Rosa, Frank L.          W49    383
Rosa, Maurice P.        N70    557
Rosaschi, Lehid         W49    383
Rose, Adam E.           N70    449
Rose, Alice             Geu    170
Rose, George Verne      N24    240
Rose, J.C., Jr.         N70   1037
Rose, John Bailey       Suc    155
Rose, Mrs. Mary G.      Bin    141
Rose, Robert E.         L73  xxiii
                        L75    xix
Roseborough, J.B.       Goo    279
Rosenbrock, Clarence Gordon
                        N24    242
Rosenbrock, Henry       N70    929
Rosenbrock, Henry J.    W49    383
Rosenbrock, John Henry
                        Dav   1171
Rosenfeld, Ben          N70    274
Rosenthal, Benjamin     Wre    437
Ross, B.F.              W31    50
Ross, George H.         W49    383
Ross, Gilbert C.        Dav   1234
        M15 (1:83); N10  (126)
                        Wre    643
Ross, John R.           W31    50
Ross, John R. (Jack)    W49    383
Ross, Orrin C.          Dav   1173
        Scr   2:51; Wre   626
Ross, R. Ian            L77    1i
Ross, Silas E.          Cur    101
        Scr   2:52; W49   384
Ross, Silas Earl        M50    48
        N70   826; Ros    51
Ross, W.K.              Elk    373
Rossi, Gabriel          Lam    288
Rosso, Martin           N70    915
Roth, Marvin H.         Phi    54
Rothrock, Joseph Trimble
                        Rei    49
Rowan, Donald E.        W49    384
Rowan, Francis C.       Scr  2:404
Rowan, Francis Chris    W49    384

Rowe, William H.     L47 Alpha
                     W49   384
Rowen, Robert A.     N70   484
Rowland, Frank (Happy)
                     Bru    28
Rowntree, Herbert E. L51 Alpha
     L53 Alpha; L59 Alpha
     L60 Alpha; L61 Alpha
Roy, Rolland F.      Dav  1177
Royle, William       Scr 2:339
Ruddell, Ruth        W49   385
Ruddell, W.C.        Per    16
                     Wre   606
Ruddell, William C.  Dav  1174
Ruddell, William C., Sr.
                     Scr 3:386
Rudiak, George       L53 Alpha
Ruedy, Clarence      L53 Alpha
                     L55    73
Rufli, Fred J., Jr.  N70   494
Rule, Richard        Moh    62
Rulison, Hattie L.   Cur    24
Ruppe, Leander Oscar (Bob)
                     Whi   557
Ruppert, Amos Roy    W49   385
Rusk, Robert F.      A82    70
          L79  lxv; L81 lxviii
Russell, Charles H.  M50    10
          N70   843; W31    50
Russell, Charles Hinton
          Chr    20; Myl   117
          N59    21; W49   385
Russell, George      Dav  1168
                     Elk   374
Russell, George B.   Ros    69
Russell, James       Wre   666
Russell, Will C.     W07    84
Rutherford, James T. Scr 2:191
Rutledge, James      Wre   579
Rutman, John         N70   507
Ruud, Robert H.      N70   421
Ryales, Percy        Lam   288
Ryan, Bob            A83    64
          A85    66; L83 xliii
                     L85   xli
Ryan, Dave M.        Wre   376
Ryan, Frank M.       Scr 3:175
Ryan, James G.       L47 Alpha
     L49 Alpha; L53 Alpha
     L57 Alpha; L59 Alpha
     L60 Alpha; W49    28
Ryan, James George   N70  1019
Ryan, James Milon    Lam   288
Ryan, Joseph R.      Wre   588
Ryan, M.E.           Wre   652
Ryan, Patrick "Patty"
                     Lam   288
Ryan, Thomas F.      Scr  3:85
                     W49   385

Sabala, Domingo      Sil   319
Sacanavino, Steven A.
                     N70   563
Sader, Robert M.     A82    72
          A83   196; A85   198
          L81  lxix; L83 lxxxi
                     L85  lxxx
Sadler, Reinhold     Chr    20
          Myl    61; N59    10
               Scr 1:383, 3:53
Sadler, Rheinhold    Haw     6
Sain, Charles M.     Wre   503
St. Clair, Raymond   Dav  1247
Salicchi, Alfred     Lam   288
Salicchi, Ceasare, Jr.
                     Lam   288
Salicchi, Ceasare, Sr.
                     Lam   289
Salicchi, Cesare     N70   422
Salicchi, Ejusto     Lam   289
Salisbury, Arthur Nelson
          Dav  1172; Jud   (13)
                     O'B   120
Salisbury, O.J.      Goo   346
Salsberry, John      W07    64
Salsburry, Jack      D15   (71)
Salter, T.J.D.       M15 (1:123)
Salter, Thomas J.D.  Dav  1171
                     O'B   120
Salvi, Joseph J.     N70   381
Sampson, Harry       Rei   147
Sampson, Jim         Geo   304
Samuels, William L.  Dav  1176
                     Scr 2:184
Sanders, J.A.        N10 (140)
Sanders, John A.     M32    23
          O'B   120; Scr 2:37
Sanders, John Adams  M15 (2:37)
                     W31    50
Sanders, W.B.        Ang   411
Sanders, Wilbur F.   Goo   326
Sandquist, Ernest F. "Sandy"
                     N70   369
Sanford, _____      Lam   289
Sanford, Clifford    L57 Alpha
Sanford, George L.   Dav  1180
          Lab    63; M15 (1:115)
          M32    37; Scr 2:329
                     W49   385
Sanford, George Leonard
          M50    40; O'B   121
Sanford, Graham      W31    50
Sanford, J.M.        Ang   371
Sanford, John        W49   385
Sanford, Leslie M.   Ros    72
San Pedro, Manuel
          Ang   Facing 141
Sans, Edward R.      Scr 2:242
Saralegui, Antonio   Sil   398
Sarman, Edwin Carl   N70   911
Sarmen, Fred         Dav  1180
Sauder, Irus         Lam   289

Sauer, Andrew            Ang    624
            Scr 2:305; Was    329
                         Wre    483
Sauer, Frank J.          Scr 3:354
Sauer, George            Scr 3:202
Sauer, Leo Frank         N70    822
Sauer, Louis A.          Scr 3:201
Sauer, William F.        Scr 3:355
Saunders, John Olin      Dav   1181
Saunders, Wiltshire      Wre    352
Savage, David E.         Whi    277
Savage, Gladys Whitehead
                         Whi    387
Savage, Leslie Loring
                         W07    162
Saval, Joe               Sil    313
Saval, John              Gra     60
                         Sil    313
Saval, Joseph            N70    471
Saviers, Claude E.       W49    386
Saviers, Claude Emmett
                         W31     51
Saviers, H.E.            W31     51
Saviers, Harry E.        Scr 2:291
Saviers, Henry E.        Dav   1181
Sawyer, Mrs. Bette       N70    188
Sawyer, F. Grant         Chr     20
Sawyer, Frank Grant      Myl    123
Sawyer, Grant            Cro    124
            N59    22; N70    185
Saxton, Orieal           N70    232
Sayer, John T.           N24    243
Sayre, Andrew C.         N70    973
Sayre, John H.           M88     32
Sbragia, Joseph John W49    386
Scanavino, Louis Gregg
                         N24    244
Scanavino, Steve A.      N70    563
Scanlan, Rev. Lawrence
                         Gor     21
Scanlan, Martin J.       M32    157
            Scr 2:174; W49    386
Scanland, Martin J.      W31     51
Scatena, Louis John      N70    965
Sceirine, Ceges "Jack"
                         N70    951
Sceirine, Jack Duane N70    972
Sceirine, Lester         N70   1043
Schacht, Ethel Nell      N70    860
Schadler, Andreas J. Scr 2:283
Schadler, Frederick M.
                         Scr 2:282
Schaeffer, Robert H. Scr 2:428
Schaffer, George         Wre    642
Schank, L.C.             L57 Alpha
Scheel, Robert C.        Wre    529
Scheeline, Harry H.      Scr 2:117
                         W31     51
Scheeline, Moritz    M15 (2:61)
                         Scr 2:115
Schenck, Gretta J.       N70   1050
Schindler, A. Ross   W49    386

Schloerb, Edwin W.       N70    276
Schmidt, Henry C.        Dav   1181
            Scr 3:150; W49    386
Schmidtlein, Mrs. Henry
                         Bru     20
Schmithen, Charley       Gra     58
Schmitt, Edward          Scr 2:216
Schneider, F.J.          Wre    538
Schneider, Robert J. Phi     54
Schnitzer, William H.
                         N10   (184)
Schoer, Claus            Wre    556
Schofield, Della         Arr     60
Schofield, Jack          L73    xli
                         L75   xlii
Schofield, Jack L.       L73 xxxii
                         L75    xxx
Schofield, Jack Lund N70    398
Schofield, James W.      A82     74
            A83    136; A85    138
            L77    li; L81    lxx
            L83 lxxxii; L85 lxxxi
Schofield, Merle F.      N70    209
Schoolroy, Ross          Lam    289
Schouweiler, Robert L.
            L59 Alpha; L60 Alpha
                         L61 Alpha
Schrader, Erich Julius
                         W49    386
Schroeder, Elmer F.      N70   1037
Schultz, Ernest A.       Moh     41
Schultz, George          M78     61
Schultz, Otto T.         Scr 3:224
Schultz, Ruth            Phi     55
Schultz, William E.      Phi     55
Schuman, William C.      L47 Alpha
Schumann, George Amos
                         N70    629
Schwab, Charles M.       W07     61
Schwaikert, Harry        D15    (75)
Schwamb, Martin G.       W49    387
Schwartz, Mrs. Louise
                         N70    935
Schwartz, Otto Frederick
    (Fritz)               N70    307
Schwartz, Rudolph        N70    936
Schwarzschild, Julius
                         M15 (1:131)
Scott, A.L.              Scr 2:429
Scott, A.W.              Ske    281
Scott, Eddie B.          N70    915
Scott, Edward L.         Dav   1206
Scott, Emma J.           Scr 2:367
Scott, Felix A.          N70    554
Scott, Fred Willie       N24    245
Scott, Harvey W.         Goo    352
Scott, James             Scr 3:341
                         Wre    402
Scott, Joseph            Elk    375
            Hal    97; Lam    290
                         W49    387
Scott, Kenneth Dee       N70    485

Smith, T.B.   Ang   413
Smith, Talmage L.   W31   54
Smith, Thor   Bru   19
Smith, Timmons S.   N70   517
Smith, W.T.   Lam   294
Smith, William   Moh   39
Smith, William Frank   N70   298
Smith, William Harold
   N70   991
Smith, Zina   Whi   311
Smyth, John   Moh   67
Smyth, Roy Melvin   N24   258
Snare, Ferney George   N24   260
Snell, Henry (Hank)   Lam   294
Snelson, Joseph E.   Scr 2:160
Snooks, _____   Lam   295
Snow, Orrin   Whi   256
Snyder, Charles   Wre   585
Snyder, Eddie Roland   N70   892
Snyder, Fred W.   W49   395
Snyder, Frederic   Scr 2:348
Snyder, Jerry C.   W49   395
Snyder, Joel T.   W49   395
Snyder, Willard F.   D07   (77)
Snyder, William E.   W49   395
Somers, Peter J.   Dav   1241
   N10   (60); O'B   122
Somerville, William T.
   Dav   1241
Sommer, Clarence E.   L47   Alpha
Sonne, Charles Frederick
   Rei   55
Sonne, Ole H.   Dav   1242
Sopp, George   Dav   1180
Sorensen, Douglas   N70   982
Sorensen, Fred C.   W49   395
Sorensen, Harold A.   N70   222
Sorensen, John   Whi   608
Sorensen, John M.   Whi   606
Sorensen, Martina   Whi   614
Sorensen, Von Loyd   N70   526
Sorenson, Lloyd   Lam   295
Souter, Clyde D.   M32   79
   M50   84
Souter, Clyde Douglas
   W49   395
Southward, Mrs. Joan   Bin   141
Southworth, Charles E.
   Scr 2:463
Southworth, George   Dav   1242
Southworth, George A.
   W49   396
Southworth, George A., Jr.
   W49   396
Southworth, George A., Sr.
   N70   908
Southworth, George Arvin, Sr.
   M50   94
Southworth, Stoddard   Scr 2:461
Souza, Maurice Joseph
   N70   594
Spain, Galen Jerome   N70   619

Spann, Mrs. Harriet Gaddis
   Bin   141
Spann, Harriett G.   Scr 2:269
Sparks, Elbert H.   W49   396
Sparks, John   Chr   20
   Elk   380; Myl   67
   N07   54; N59   11
   Scr 1:411; W07   33
   Wre   313
Spaulding, John C.   Lam   295
Specter, Fred   Lam   295
Spencer, A   Dav   1242
   Wre   664
Spencer, Guy A.   Dav   1243
Spencer, John   Gra   49
   Wre   749
Spencer, Louis B.   Scr 3:476
Sperry, William A.   Ang   457
Spindel, Stephen   Wre   636
Spinner, William   Wre   592
Spinney, George R.   M88   38
Spradling, G.B.   W31   55
Spragg, W.H.   Ang   418
Sprague, Charles S.   D07   (76)
   D15   (69); M15   (2:15)
   W07   170
Sprague, Charles Silvey
   Dav   1243
Spratling, William Max
   N70   503
Spriggs, Gaylyn J.   A85   210
   L85   lxxxiii
Spring, Edward S.   M78   51
Springmeyer, Charles H.
   Dav   1248
Springmeyer, Frederick C.
   Dav   1249
Springmeyer, George   Dav   1245
   M15   (1:53); M32   65
   M50   78; N10   (160)
   N70   852; O'B   123
   W31   55; W49   396
Springmeyer, Jeffry E.
   W49   396
Springmeyer, Leonard   Dav   1252
Springmeyer, Melvin Frederick
   N70   907
Sproule, C.H.   Wre   468
Squires, _____   Lam   296
Squires, Charles P.   W49   397
Squires, Delphine   Geu   135
Squires, Delphine Anderson
   Ame   347
Squires, Ronald E.   Phi   57
Stadelman, Richard R.
Stadtfeld, Jacob, Jr.
   M88   25
Stadtherr, Anthony L.
   Scr 2:153; W49   397
Stadtmuller, Fred   Dav   1248
Stampfli, Maynard M.   M32   145

Stampley, Orville Knighten
                       Moh    70
Stanford, Leland      Goo    20
Stanislawsky, Henry  N10  (92)
Stanley, Carle B.    W49   397
Stanley, Louise H.   N70   643
Stanton, Daniel      Mea    95
Stanton, Thaddeus H. Goo   311
Stanton, W.A.       D07  (74)
Stanton, William Augustus
                       Suc   100
Stark, C.B., Sr.    L55    74
Stark, Clyde B.     N70   300
Starks, George A.   L47 Alpha
Starr, Ronald Lawrence
                       N70   568
States, Walter Lincoln
                       W49   398
St. Clair, Raymond   Dav  1247
Stead, James E.     N70   822
Stebbins, John F.    W07   248
Steele, Charles Curwin
                       W49   398
Steele, Harriet      Scr 3:462
Steele, Robert       Scr 3:462
                       Wre   445
Steele, Robert M.    Wre   545
Steffan, Albert      Dav  1249
Steffes, Peter       Dav  1249
Steinbach, Charles F.
                       W31    55
Steinmetz, Frank J.  Wre   358
Steinmetz, Theodore J.
                       Ros    42
Steinmiller, George C.
        Scr 2:185; W49   398
Steneri, Donald R.   N70   605
Steninger, Corda Barrett
                       Geu   139
Steninger, Melvin    Lam   296
Stenovich, Edith     W49   398
Stenovich, Frank A.  W49   399
Stenovich, Leland Leroy
                       N70   514
Stenson, Roger P.    Dav  1250
Stephens, Frederick  N70   315
Stephens, William T., Jr.
                       N70   426
Stephenson, William P.
                       W31    55
Stern, Joseph H.     Dav  1250
Stetler, Byron F.    Phi    57
Stetson, George       W49   399
Stetson, W.W.        M88    38
Stevenot, Archie D.  Bix   139
Stevens, Ed         Bru     9
Stevens, Frank A.    Dav  1251
      O'B   123; Scr  3:20
Stevens, Gene        Bru     8
Stevens, Harold     Bru     8
Stevens, Howard R.   W49   399
Stevens, Jim        Bru     8

Stevens, Winnie     Bru     8
Stevenson, C.C.     Scr 1:339
Stevenson, Charles C.
      Ban   321; Chr   21
                       N59     6
Stevenson, Charles Clark
                       Myl    37
Stever, Charles     Dav  1251
Stever, Verne R.     N70   207
Stewart,             Lam   296
Stewart, Artimesia   N70   212
Stewart, B.W. Robert Burwell
                       Elk   398
Stewart, Cyril D.    N70   288
Stewart, Daniel Segmiller
                       N70   229
Stewart, David Levi  N70   235
Stewart, E.A.        D15  (73)
Stewart, Frank       Goo   192
Stewart, Frank S.    N70   870
Stewart, Gerald R.   L47 Alpha
Stewart, Harry E.    Dav  1251
                       Scr 2:245
Stewart, Harry Emanuel
                       W49   399
Stewart, Helen J.    Scr 3:464
Stewart, Helen Jane Wiser
                       Ame   346
Stewart, Howard R.   W49   399
Stewart, J. Frank    Scr 2:246
Stewart, J. Wesley   Dav  1252
Stewart, Janson F.   A82    76
      A83   142; L79  lxvi
      L81 lxix; L83 lxxxiv
Stewart, Jesse L.    N70   237
Stewart, Joseph      Chu    12
Stewart, Leslie John N70   598
Stewart, Marion King N70   218
Stewart, Mrs. Oline J.
                       Cur    79
Stewart, R.B.        Lam   296
Stewart, Richard A.  Cro   130
Stewart, Robert      W31    55
Stewart, S. Grant    Cro   132
Stewart, Sumner Kent N70   270
Stewart, William Franklin
                       Moh    28
Stewart, William J.  Scr 3:467
Stewart, William M.  Ban   174
      Goo   140; M78    30
      M88    29; O'B    65
Stewart, William Morris
      Chr    21; N09    45
      Scr 1:232; Shu   635
Stewart, William Thomas
                       N70   210
Stimler, Harry C.    D07  (75)
                       W07   134
Stinson, A.J.        M15 (2:25)
Stinson, Andrew J.   M32   153
Stinson, William      Lam   296
Stitser, Avery D.    W49   399

Stitser, Rollin C.    W31    55
Stock, Charles        Lam   296
Stock, Frank          Lam   297
Stock, Orvis          Lam   297
Stock, Wenzel J., Jr.
                      Dav  1216
Stock, Wenzl J., Jr.  Scr 3:497
Stock, Wilbourne      N24   261
Stock, William        Ang   458
Stockbridge, _____   Lam   297
Stocker, Mayme Virginia
                      Cro   134
Stocks, Harrison Sidney
         N70   240; W49   400
Stoddard, Charles     Moh    70
Stoddard, Charles H.  Dav  1246
Stoddard, Richard C.  Jud   (14)
         M15 (1:37); O'B   123
Stodiek, Wilbur H.    W49   400
Stoffer, Fred         Lam   297
Stoker, Clarence H.   N70   194
Stoker, George S.     Per    76
Stoker, Hiram         Dav  1246
Stone, Ermon L.       W49   400
Stone, Henry A.       Dav  1247
Stone, James A.       A83   190
         A85   192; L83 lxxxv
                      L85 lxxxiv
Stone, M.N.           Ang   570
Stone, Thomas N.      Ang   224
Stone, Walter Corbaley
                      W07   142
Stone, Wm. F.N.       Moh    28
Storey, Edward Fairs  Ang   569
Storey, Edward Faris  Ban   215
                      Tay   117
Stotler, Marsh        Lam   297
Stover, Ernest Jefferson
                      N24   262
Strange, Frank        Lam   298
Stratton, Ed          Mur   310
Stratton, Francis A.  Suc   145
Stratton, John H.     N70   835
Streeter, John Bernard
                      M50 144-F
Streeter, Oscar       Lam   298
Streeter, Randolph    Lam   298
Streeter, Richard Lee
                      N70   629
Streeter, Sylvester M.
                      Lam   298
Streshley, Joe        G85     5
                      Mur   151
Streshley, Lena E.    Scr 3:263
Streshley, Leroy A.   N70   989
Streshley, Tucker     Scr 3:262
Stringham, A. Clyde   W31    56
Stringham, Clyde      Lam   298
Stringham, Sabra      Whi   373
Strosnider, Fred      L49 Alpha
         L51 Alpha; N70   944
                      W49  23; 400

Strosnider, Ruth Barry
                      N70   948
Strothers, Enoch      Ros    24
Strouse, Mark         Ang   570
Stuard, James         Dav  1247
Stuart, R. La Mont    N70   525
Stubbs, Joseph E.     Scr  2:71
Stubbs, Joseph Edward
         Dav  1216; Wre   570
Sturgeon, Raymond L.  N70   439
Sturtevant, James     Was   205
Sullivan, Bat         Dav  1216
Sullivan, Daniel J.   Dav  1217
                      M32   139
Sullivan, James       Ang   642
Sullivan, John J.     Dav  1218
                      M15 (1:121)
Sullivan, Maurice J.
         M15 (1:77); M32    89
                      Scr  3:67
Sullivan, Maurice Joseph
                      M50    58
Sullivan, Ruth Davis  N70   625
Summerfield, Alexander
                      Wre   431
Summerfield, G.W.     Wre   653
Summerfield, Lester D.
         Bix   155; M32    49
         Scr 2:118; W31    56
Summerfield, Lester Douglas
         M15 (2:59); M50    44
                      W49   400
Summerfield, Marie Louise
                      Scr  2:56
Summerfield, Sardis   O'B   123
         Scr  2:56; Wre   608
Summerfield, Sol Milton
                      W31    56
Summerfield, Solomon M.
                      Scr 3:241
Summers, Edith Robertson
                      N70   842
Summers, James        Whi   606
Summers, Sadie        Whi   606
Summers, Thomas       Scr 3:424
Sundberg, J.F.        W31    56
Sundeen, Stanley Daniel
                      Ros    88
Sunderland, John      N10   (34)
Sunstedt, Nellie      Scr 3:421
Supp, Albert D.       W49   401
Supp, Albert Dewey    N70   462
Supp, Carl C.         N70  1042
Sustacha, Jess        Lam   298
Sustacha, Jose, Jr.   Lam   299
Sustacha, Jose, Sr.   Hal   116
                      Lam   299
Sutherland, George    Scr 3:124
Sutherland, John (Jack)
         McPherson     N70   486
Sutherland, William   Dav  1212
                      Wre   608

71

Sutro, Adolph             Chr      25
         Goo    240;  M78      67
                      M88      27
Sutter, John A.           Goo       7
Sutton, Ingeborg R.       Scr   3:163
Sutton, John E.           Scr   3:161
Suverkrup, Arthur N.  W49      401
Suverkrup, John W.    W49      401
Swackhamer, William D.
         L47 Alpha;  L49 Alpha
         L51 Alpha;  L53 Alpha
         L55     74;  L57 Alpha
         L59 Alpha;  L60 Alpha
         L61 Alpha;  L63 Alpha
Swain, Courtenay C.   A83      184
         A85    186;  L83 lxxxvi
         L85 lxxxv;  W49      29
Swallow, George N.    W49      401
Swallow, Grover       N70      341
Swallow, R.T.         W31      56
Swallow, Richard T.   Scr   3:267
Swallow, Richard Thomas
                      N70      198
Swanson, Harry        W31      57
Swanson, Harry B.     L59 Alpha
         L60 Alpha;  L61 Alpha
                      L63 Alpha
Swanson, Henry Emanuel
                      W49      401
Swanson, Merle W.     N70      570
Swartz, George L.     Ros      62
Sweatt, John E.       Scr   2:277
Sweatt, John Eugene   W49      402
Swedberg, Walter G.   N24      264
Sweeney, E.D.         Dav     1211
Sweeney, James G.     Dav     1210
         O'B    124;  Wre      383
Sweeney, Minor Major  W49      402
Sweetland, _____     Lam      299
Sweetser, Frank D.    Scr    2:87
Sweringer, Samuel E.  Lam      299
Swett, Clarence C♂    W49      402
Swett, Clarence Charles
                      N70      548
Swobe, Coe            L63 Alpha
                      L73    xxii
Sykes, C.P.           M78      58
Symmes, Whitman       Dav     1190
                      M15   (2:21)
Syphus, Christiana Long
                      Mea      229
Syphus, Clara Melissa
                      Mea      236
Syphus, Edward Henry  Mea      232
Syphus, George Alvin  Mea      233
Syphus, Levi Walter   Mea      234
Syphus, Lovina        Mea      234
Syphus, Luke          Mea      229


Taber, E.J.L.         W31      57


Taber, Erroll James Livingston
         Dav   1191;  O'B      124
Taber, Harold O.      Jud     (21)
                      W49      403
Taber, Henry Stanley  W49      402
Taber, James Henry    Wre      381
Taber, Milo           L47 Alpha
                      N70      493
Tadich, John V.       Ete       9
Taggert, Frank G.     Mur      94
Talbot, George F.     Lab      64
         M15 (1:57);  O'B      124
Talbot, George Frederick
         Dav   1188;  Wre      392
Talbot, George Fredrick
                      Lam      300
Talbot, Henry M.      Lam      300
Talbot, Mary E.       Cur      63
Talley, Melville O.   N24      266
Tallman, A.V.         L47 Alpha
         L49 Alpha;  L51 Alpha
                      W49      23
Tallman, Clay         Dav     1191
                      O'B      125
Tally, Milo L.        W49      403
Tamblyn, Alfred D.    Scr   2:288
         W31     57;  W49      403
Tamka, Harold W.      W49      403
Tanner, Darrell D.    L79     lxvi
Tasem, Mrs. Pauline   Cur      80
Taylor, Alyce Savage  Phi      58
Taylor, Barbara M.    Phi      58
Taylor, C.D.          Suc      108
Taylor, Claude Lee    N70      477
Taylor, Edwin B.      W49      403
Taylor, Francis       N70     1023
Taylor, George W.     Lam      300
Taylor, Harrie L.     D07     (79)
Taylor, Harry Leslie  Suc      109
Taylor, I.M.          M78      74
Taylor, J. Minor      Ang      611
Taylor, John G.       Geo      367
                      Per  35,  45
Taylor, John Gilmore  Elk      399
Taylor, Lillie Ann (Leslie)
                      Tay      95
Taylor, Maude Sawin   Tay      vii
                      W49      404
Taylor, Neil E.       N24      268
Taylor, O.F.          Wre      444
Taylor, Robert H.     Ang      579
                      Goo      218
Taylor, Robert M.     N70      358
Taylor, Ryland G.     Scr   3:181
                      W49      404
Taylor, Ward E.       Scr   2:257
Taylor, William       N24      270
Taylor, William Benjamin
                      Moh      24
Tebbs, Terry          A85      228
                      L85 lxxxvi

Tedford, John N., Jr.
                      W49    404
Tedford, Kenneth H.   N70    323
Tedford, May H.       Cur     94
Teebe, Stanley        W49    404
Tees, John            W31     57
Teixeira, Antonio Pimentel
                      N24    272
Temoke, Frank, Jr.    N70    506
Tenente, Antonio Fraetes
                      N24    274
Tennant, Ray          Phi     58
Tennille, James B.    N70    208
Terrell, Clyde R.     L47  Alpha
          L49 Alpha;  W49     29
Terry, Eliza Jane Pulsipher
                      Mea    236
Terry, Ellen          Whi    259
Terry, Emma Jane      Whi    554
Terry, George Alphonzo
                      Whi    384
Terry, Marilda
          Whi    569, 578, 609
Terry, Mary           Whi    561
Terry, Mary Ellen     Whi    319
Terry, Otis           Whi    349
Terry, Otis Merlin    N70    376
Terry, Susie M.       Whi    349
Terry, Veda           Whi    395
Terry, William Alanson
                      Whi    324
Terwilliger, Cecil D.
                      D15    (77)
Terzi, John G.        N24    276
Testolin, Antonio Paul
                      N70    247
Testolin, Tony        N70   1039
Tevis, Lloyd          M78     34
Thacher, William M.   W49    405
Thacker, Oscar Leroy  N70    396
Thatcher, George B.   Dav   1190
          M32    15; N10   (182)
                      Scr  2:204
Thatcher, George Bayard
          M50    20; O'B    125
                      W49    405
Thatcher, John P.     W49    405
Thatcher, John Pemberton
                      M50  144-H
Thatcher, LeRoy       M15  (2:79)
Thaxter, George C.    Ang    559
Thayer, Rufus C.      W07    158
Theelen, Henry        Ang    371
Thoma, George H.      Scr   3:86
                      Wre    658
Thomas, Bob           A83    211
          A85    213; L83 lxxxvii
                      L85 lxxxvii
Thomas, C.C.          Ang    511
Thomas, Evans Whitcomb
                      W07    148

Thomas, Helen Marye
          Gra Preface; N70  1005
Thomas, Horace Samuel "Chic"
                      N70    449
Thomas, Ruby Schroeder
                      N70    480
Thomas, W.H.          W31     57
Thomas, William       Wre    432
Thomas, William H.    Dav   1271
                      W49    405
Thomas, William O.    Dav   1271
Thomas, William R.    Dav   1272
          O'B    126; Scr  2:493
Thompson, Alice L.    Scr  2:208
Thompson, Andy        N70    371
Thompson, Bruce R.    W49    405
Thompson, Charles A.  W49    405
Thompson, Danny L.    A82     78
          A83    163; A85    165
          L81    lxx; L83 lxxxviii
                      L85 lxxxviii
Thompson, Dianthus    Whi    570
Thompson, Florence Bryant
                      Geu     80
Thompson, Florence M.
                      Scr  2:206
Thompson, George F.    Scr  3:486
Thompson, Gordon R.   W49    406
Thompson, Grace G.    Scr  3:458
Thompson, Henry       Lam    300
Thompson, Hyrum       W49    406
Thompson, I.S.        O'B    126
                      Scr  3:392
Thompson, Isaac S.    Suc    106
Thompson, Jack Guy    O'B    126
Thompson, John Grey M15  (2:91)
                      Suc    105
Thompson, John W.     Lam    300
Thompson, M.S.        Ang    455
Thompson, Marinus     Whi    570
Thompson, Mathew Stanley
                      Moh     37
Thompson, Reuben C.H.
                      Scr   3:90
Thompson, Snow-Shoe   Tay     59
Thompson, Thea C.     Scr  2:265
Thompson, Theodore M.
                      N70   1005
Thompson, William     Scr  2:207
                      Was     93
Thomsen, Roy D.       N70    508
Thorn, Raymond Earl   W49    406
Thorne, Marco Gerson  W49    406
Thornton, Byron O.    W49    406
Thornton, Harry I.    Goo    207
                      O'B     70
Thorpe, John          Lam    300
Thorpe, Margaret      Wre    457
Thorpe, Moreton J.    W49    407
Thrall, Charles Edward
                      N24    277
Thran, Richard        Dav   1272

Thrasher, Helen Clare
       N70 849
Threlkel, John E.  Dav 1272
   Scr 2:110; W49 407
Thuesen, Chris   N70 807
Thurston, Harmon L. N70 587
Tibbals, Don H.   N70 995
Tiberti, J.A.    Cro 136
Tiberti, Jelindo A. W49 407
Tidestrom, Ivar Frederick
       Rei 107
Tilden, Augustus  O'B 127
Tillim, Sidney Joseph
       W49 407
Tinker, Dorothy   Cro 138
Tinker, Dorothy E.  N70 276
Tinnin, John    W07 185
Tippett, John    Geo 294
Tippett, Samuel R.  M32 117
    Scr 2:199; W31 57
Tipton, Hugh K.   N70 807
Titlow, Emerson F.  N70 921
Tobin, Clement L.  Dav 1273
       Scr 2:85
Tobin, Phil M.   W49 407
Tobin, Phil Metschan N70 853
Tobin, W.J.    D15 (83)
Tobin, William J.  Scr 3:239
Togniotti, Domenico N24 278
Tognoni, Baptista  L53 Alpha
       L55 74
Tognoni, Elmo V.  N70 625
Tognoni, Joe    D07 (80)
Tolladay, Yolanda Smith
       N70 585
Tolley, J.B.    Ang 398
Tomera, Edward V.  Lam 301
Tomlinson, J.A.   L49 Alpha
Tomlinson, John G.  W49 29
Tomlinson, W.H. Joe N70 369
Tompkins, C. Alton  W31 58
Tonkin, George    Bru 21
Tonkin, Walter J.  Wre 325
Tool, Elizabeth   Bru 22
Tooley, Bert Theodore
       N70 515
Torrence, Carl W.  Cur 115
Torreyson, James D.  Wre 712
Torreyson, William D.
       Ang 535
Torvinen, Roy L.   L73 xliii
Townsend, Randolph J.
  A83 86; A85 88
  L83 xliv; L85 xliii
Townsend, Randolph John
       Phi 58
Tracy, Frank A.   W49 407
Tracy, Frank Alton  M50 76
Train, Agnes    Rei 127
Train, Percy    Rei 127
Trankle, Hellen G.  W49 408
Trathen, E. Russell W31 58

Trathen, Edward R.  Scr 3:133
Traver, Fred W.   W49 408
Travers, Cecil J.  W31 58
Treadway, Aaron D.  Ang 533
Trelease, Harold (Bill)
       N70 413
Trembath, Nona Roberts
       N70 397
Tremewan, Charles Sydney
       N70 533
Tremewan, Oliver R. N70 410
Trent, Walter E.   D15 (79)
Trento, Pete    Lam 302
Trescartes, Albert  Lam 301
Trescartes, Charles M.
       Lam 301
Trescartes, Gerald  Lam 301
Trescartes, Victoria P.
       Lam 301
Tresnit, Milan Joseph
       Phi 59
Treweek, Nicholas  D07 (78)
Trianovich, Nikol  Ete 131
Trimble, Robert A.  Scr 3:493
Triplett, Charles J. W49 408
Triplett, F.H.   Wre 529
Triplett, J.F.   Wre 399
Triplett, Joseph F.  Lam 302
Triplett, Phil S.  Wre 461
Tripple, Patricia A. Phi 59
Tritle, Lloyd H.  Cro 140
Trittle, Lloyd H.  W49 408
Trosi, Charles A.  Scr 2:341
Trosi, Marie G.   Scr 2:342
Trost, Holger    Lam 303
Trott, Harry    Lam 303
Troupe, Claude Raymond
       N70 352
Trousdale, Atwell F. Wre 667
Trout, Len L., Jr.  Phi 60
Truckee     Ban 217
Trueman, Edward   Lam 303
Truett, Velma Stevens
       N70 189
Truman, Olive    W49 408
Trumbell, Margaret  W49 409
Tsukamoto, Thomas S. N70 536
Tubman, Father T.M.
     M15 (1:109)
Tubman, Thomas M.  Scr 2:379
Tucker, Robert W.  Dav 1273
Tucker, Thomas T., Jr.
       Phi 60
Turano, Anthony Mario
       W49 409
Turley, Mae Alger  N70 202
Turnbaugh, Isaac   Mea 239
Turner, Bert M.   Lam 303
Turner, Collier   Whi 586
Turner, David H.   L51 Alpha
Turner, Delos A.   M32 101
       Scr 2:200

Vignola, Fred             Lam    305
Vignola, Joe              Lam    305
Vignola, John             Lam    305
Vignola, Sam              Lam    305
Vincent, Fern A.          W49    411
Vincent, Raymond E.       W49    411
Virgin, D.W.              O'B    128
Vizina, Earl G.           N70    309
Vocovich, Sam             Ete    129
Voight, Fred C.           Dav   1269
Voight, Fred G.           Lam    305
Voight, Harry G.          Lam    305
Voight, Henrich (Henry)
                          Lam    306
Vollmar, Adolph           N24    286
Vollmar, Harry            N24    287
Von Tobel, Ed, Sr.        Cro    144
Von Tobel, Edward         W49    411
Von Tobel, Edward J.      W49    412
Von Tobel, George         L53  Alpha
          L55    75;  L57 Alpha
                          L61  Alpha
Von Tobel, George W.      W49    412
Von Tobel, Jacob E.       W49    412
Von Tobel, Jake           L63  Alpha
Voss, Wilfred T.          Ros     76
Vucanovich, Mitchel       Ete    110
Vucovich, Spiro           Ete    138


Wadsworth, Benjamin Franklin
                          Mea    260
Wadsworth, Bessie Mathews
                          Mea    259
Wadsworth, Carl Eugene
                          Mea    258
Wadsworth, David T.       Mea    259
Wadsworth, Eliza J.       Scr  3:518
Wadsworth, Eliza Jane Terry
                          Mea    248
Wadsworth, Franklin E.
                          Scr  2:425
Wadsworth, Franklin Earl
                          N70    957
Wadsworth, Franklin Ernest
          Mea    250; W31    58
Wadsworth, George A. Mea    243
Wadsworth, J.L.           L49  Alpha
Wadsworth, James Allen
                          Mea    246
Wadsworth, James Allen, II
                          Mea    252
Wadsworth, James L.       W49     29
Wadsworth, James Leo N70    207
Wadsworth, Lawrence  Mea    255
Wadsworth, Leonard E.
                          N70    245
Wadsworth, Milton Lafayette
                          Mea    256
Wadsworth, Nephi J.  Scr  3:518

Wadsworth, Nephi John
                          Mea    247
Wadsworth, Nephi John, Jr.
                          Mea    249
Wagner, Harry H.          N70    577
Wagner, Sue               A82    123
          A83     88; A85     90
          L75  liii; L77   liii
          L79 lxviii; L81     xl
          L83    xlv; L85    xlv
Wainwright, Max R.        L55     75
Waite, Curtis B.          Cro    146
Waite, Roy                W49    412
Wakeling, Allen           Whi    352
Wakeling, Ellen           Whi    402
Wakeling, Lillian         Whi    317
Waldman, Herbert H.       W49    412
Waldo, Gilbert B.         Wre    515
Walker, Charles A.        Dav   1269
Walker, Charles Ashley
                          O'B    129
Walker, Clive Arden       N24    288
Walker, Edgar H.          Dav   1276
                          Scr 2:236
Walker, Edgar Harlowe
                          W31     59
Walker, Francis Clemons, Jr.
                          Mea    261
Walker, John P.           Lam    307
Walker, Lee E.            L73    xxii
                          L75 xxxiii
Walker, M. Rollin    Scr 2:168
Walker, Raymond Curtis
                          Cur    153
Walker, T. Schmaling W49    413
Walker, William A.        Ang    630
Walker, William J.        W49    413
Wall, E.A.                D07    (86)
Wall, William S.          O'B    129
Wallace, Charles          Moh     65
Wallace, Dave             Esm     39
Wallace, Florence Kent
                          N70    353
Wallace, George Leonard
                          N70    531
Wallace, J.D.             W31     59
Wallace, James D.         Scr 3:412
Wallace, Joseph A.        Scr 3:290
Wallace, Richard Ted W31     59
Walsh, J. Emmett          D15    (89)
          Dav   1277; O'B    129
Walsh, J. Herbert         Scr 3:245
Walsh, John Charles  W49    413
Walsh, Patrick            Scr 2:400
Walter, Rose Elizabeth
    Goldbach               N70    920
Walters, F.E.             L51  Alpha
                          L53  Alpha
Walters, F.E. "Pete" Lam    307
Walthall, Harris          Suc    133
Walther, Jack        Hal 108, 118
                          Lam    307

Walther, Joe              Hal    117
                         Lam    308
Walti, Elsie             G85     10
Walti, Fritz             Gra  9, 15
Walts, Guy W.            W49    413
Wanderer, Emile N.       W49    413
Wankier, Lorena          Whi    613
Wampler, Reece B.        D07    (85)
Ward, Albert M.          Wre    687
Ward, Albert W.          Cur    119
Ward, Arthur             Bru     26
Ward, James              Lam    308
Ward, Margaret R.        N70    194
Wardin, Anna H.          Cur     32
Wardin, Elmer E.         Scr  2:284
Wardle, Austin           Cur     83
Wardle, Austin Robert
                         N70    948
Wardle, Mrs. Luella      Cur     84
Warmbath, Samuel M.      D07    (84)
Warner, Edward Raynsford
                         Chu     13
Warner, Paul W.          L47  Alpha
       L49 Alpha;  L51  Alpha
                         W49     29
Warnock, Nettie P        Whi    596
Warren, Mrs. Anna        Cur     29
Warren, Anna M.          O'B    129
                         Scr  2:389
Warren, Charles D.       Wre    581
Warren, Donald Jerome
                         N70    537
Warren, Olive Ogilvie
                         Cur    139
Warren, Richard P. (Dick)
                         W49    413
Warren, Wallace D.       W49    414
Warsaw, E.R.             M78     62
Washburn, Daniel A.      N70    243
Washkow, Edward          W49    414
Wasson, Warren H.        Ang    533
Waterman, Augustus       M88     28
Waterman, Thomas A.      Lam    308
Waters, Richard L., Jr.
                         W49    414
Waters, Richard L., Sr.
       L53 Alpha;  L55     76
       L57 Alpha;  L59  Alpha
       L60 Alpha;  L61  Alpha
                         W49    414
Watkins, Walter S.       W49    415
Watson, H.M.             W31     59
Watson, Harry M.         W49    415
Watson, Sereno           Rei     45
Watson, William C.       W31     60
Watson, William Clarke
                         Ros     70
Watson, William H.       M78     50
                         M88     35
Watt, George             Moh     53
Weathers, Leland Stanford
                         N70    534

Weathers, Stanford       Hal     83
Weathers, William M.     W49    415
Weathers, William W.     W31     60
Weathers, William Wray
                         Hal     82
Weatherss, William M.
                         Dav   1277
Weaver, David            Geo    299
Weaver, John             Geo    299
Weaver, Ray R.           W49    415
Weaver, Willard          Lam    309
Webb, Doug               L79   lxix
Webb, Joseph Stafford
                         N24    290
Weber, Henry             D07    (83)
                         W07    128
Weber, John, Sr.         Scr  3:284
Webster, A.G.            Scr  3:408
Webster, George W.       Scr  3:305
Webster, Gertrude        Scr  3:306
Webster, Hannah E.       Scr  2:474
Webster, Ida Gertrude Willis
                         Geu    133
Webster, Stella N.       Scr  2:475
Webster, William         Scr  2:472

Wedekind, George H.      Dav   1275
          Scr   3:80; Wre    576
Wedertz, Charles E.      Scr  3:490
Wedertz, Clarence R.     Scr  3:349
Wedertz, Louis           Scr  3:488
Wedertz, Ludowig E.W.
                         Scr  3:488
Wedge, John William      Mea    263
Wedge, Virgil H.         W49    415
Weeks, Adolph            Lam    309
Weeks, Darrel Russell
                         N70    502
Weeks, Pansy Owens       N70   1006
Weeks, Russell S.        N70    528
Weeks, Seneca Charles
                         N70    902
Weikel, Karl Frederick
                         N70    954
Weiland Brothers         Lam    309
Weir, Jeanne E.          Geu    277
Weise, Robert L.         L75    liv
          L77   xliv; L79   lxix
Welde, Hannah Reese      Geu    208
Well, Robert             L49  Alpha
Weller, Charles L.       M78     29
Weller, John B.          Shu    515
Welles, John C.          W49    416
Wellesley, C. Arthur Scr 3:366
Wellington, Quincy Winthrop
                         Suc    142
Wells, George R.         M78     33
                         M88     28
Wells, H.G., Jr.         W49    416
Wells, Howard A.         W49    416
Wells, Joseph W.         W49    416
Wells, Robert            L49  Alpha

Wells, Robert C.            W49    416
Wells, Robert W.            W49     29
Wells, Sheldon O.           Geo    293
                            Scr  3:219
Welshon, _____             Lam    309
Wenban, Simeon              Ban    282
                            G85      2
Wengert, Cyril S.           Cro    148
                            W49    417
Wennhold, Richard           Dav   1270
Wente, Carl F.              Mid     89
Wermuth, William            Moh     30
Werner, Herman              Dav   1270
Werner, Mrs. Jennie E.
                            Cur     21
Werner, Theodore (Ted)
                            W49    417
West, Catherine             N70    813
West, Cladius Wilson Doc     92
West, Claude W.             Scr  2:138
West, Francis Myron         Dav   1261
West, Fred T.               L53  Alpha
                            W49    417
West, Harvey                Bix    171
West, Joe                   N70    281
West, John                  N70    967
West, Ray William           N70    647
West, Twain Dean            N70    514
Westall, Peggy              A82     82
          L77   liv; L79    lxx
                            L81  lxxii
Westerfield, W.J.           Haw     12
Westerfield, William Jackson
                            Mid     15
Westfall, Andrew            Dav   1265
                            Wre    686
Westfall, Elizabeth Bird
                            Geu    199
Westfall, Geryl L.          W49    417
Westguard, J.A.             Esm     33
Westlund, Andrew A.         Lam    309
Westlund, Charles           Lam    309
Westlund, Eldon             Lam    310
Westwood, Vernon H.         N70    384
Wharton, Fred O.            N70    940
Wheeler, Daniel C.          Geo    280
          Scr 2:313; Wre    594
Wheeler, Donald Ray N70    1041
Wheeler, J.P.               Moh     30
Wheeler, James Chauncey
                            W31     60
Wheeler, "Red" Frank Goo    146
Wheeler, Richard            M78     66
Wheeler, Samuel             Scr  2:220
Wheeler, "Uncle Dan" M15  (1:5)
Whipple, James Reuben
                            W49    417
Whipple, John L.            L49  Alpha
          Scr 3:523; W49     29
                            Whi    289
Whipple, Keith Murry N70    208

Whipple, Reed               Arr     62
          Cro    150; W49    418
Whipple, Rose               Whi    289
Whitacre, E.H.              Wre    502
Whitacre, Roy Marion W49    418
Whitacre, Walter            L47  Alpha
          L49 Alpha; L51  Alpha
          L53 Alpha; L55     62
          L57 Alpha; L59  Alpha
          L60 Alpha; L61  Alpha
          L63 Alpha; W49     29
Whitaker, Ozi William
                            Scr  2:265
Whitaker, W.W. (Walt)
                            Lam    310
Whitaker, Walter William
                            N70    345
Whitaker, Walter William, Jr.
                            N70    526
Whitburn, Frederick William
                            N24    292
White, Claude H.            N70    514
White, Fred L.              Dav   1260
                            M15 (1:23)
White, Hugh M.              W49    418
White, J.H.                 Scr  2:317
White, Wallace H.           W49    418
White, William              Lam    310
White, William Wallace
                            W49    418
Whitehead, Emma             Whi    401
Whitehead, Eva              Whi    408
Whitehead, Rennie           Whi    395
Whitehead, Rennie Adolphus
                            Whi    258
Whitehead, Reta             Whi    407
Whitehead, Stephen Robert
                            Dav   1263
Whiteley, George A.         M32    111
          Scr 2:128; W31     60
Whitlock, Hyrum David
                            Whi    578
Whitlock, Lee C.            N70    339
Whitman, B.C.               Goo    175
                            O'B     68
Whitman, Roy B.             N70    439
Whitmore, James P.          N70    639
Whitmore, James Pomeroy
          Cur     70; Ros    90
Whitmore, Walter H.         D07   (82)
Whitney, Arthur J.          Lam    310
Whitney, Claude Harvey
                            N70    514
Whitney, George B.          Mea    234
Whittemore, C.O.            W07    168
Whittenberg, Charles F.
                            D15   (91)
Whittlesea, Victor F.
                            Cro    152
Wholey, Clarence            Gil      7
Whyte, Thomas F.            L49  Alpha
Whyte, Thomas P.            W49     29

| | | | |
|---|---|---|---|
| Wickberg, G.E. | W31 | 60 | |
| Wiener, Louis, Jr. | W49 | 419 | |
| Wiens, Maynard "Ted" | Cro | 154 | |
| Wier, Adolphus W. | Scr | 2:374 | |
| Wier, Jeanne E. | Scr | 2:376 | |
| Wier, Jeanne Elizabeth | | | |
| Bin 141; | W31 | 61 | |
| | W49 | 419 | |
| Wiggins, Frank W. | Lam | 310 | |
| Wightman, D.M. | Ang | 371 | |
| Wightman, James Lisle | | | |
| | N70 | 247 | |
| Wilcox, Lyle W. | N70 | 597 | |
| Wilcox, Walter | W49 | 419 | |
| Wild, Albert | Wre | 727 | |
| Wilder, Loren | N70 | 372 | |
| Wildes, Asa | Esm | 7 | |
| Wildes, Frank L. | Wre | 532 | |
| Wiley, Harry | L47 | Alpha | |
| L49 Alpha; | L51 | Alpha | |
| L53 Alpha; | L55 | 62 | |
| | W49 | 23 | |
| Wiley, Robert P. | Dav | 1264 | |
| Wiley, Roland H. | Scr | 3:400 | |
| | W49 | 419 | |
| Wiley, Roland M. | W31 | 61 | |
| Wilgar, Bernard A. | W49 | 420 | |
| Wilkes, Charles S. | D07 | (87) | |
| Wilkin, Robert David | N70 | 198 | |
| Wilkins, Russell | W49 | 420 | |
| Wilkinson, Daniel Elliott | | | |
| Huger | O'B | 130 | |
| Williams, Abram | Geo | 358 | |
| Williams, Absalom B. | Wre | 380 | |
| Williams, David R. | Dav | 1264 | |
| Williams, Delbert E. | W31 | 61 | |
| Williams, "Doc" | Lam | 311 | |
| Williams, Edgar M. | N70 | 880 | |
| Williams, Edward | Wre | 668 | |
| Williams, Evan | Ban | 225 | |
| Williams, F. Yale | Ros | 86 | |
| Williams, Frank | N10 | (162) | |
| | W31 | 61 | |
| Williams, Harry J. | Scr | 3:310 | |
| Williams, Homer L. | Scr | 3:147 | |
| Williams, J.T. | Ang | 524 | |
| | Moh | 21 | |
| Williams, Joe | Gil | 35 | |
| Williams, John Steward, Jr. | | | |
| | N70 | 508 | |
| Williams, Leland | N70 | 398 | |
| Williams, Myrna | A85 | 132 | |
| | L85 | lxxxix | |
| Williams, Mrs. Neva E. | | | |
| Cur 92; | W49 | 420 | |
| Williams, Otto T. | Dav | 1265 | |
| | Cur | 136 | |
| Williams, Otto Thompson | | | |
| | W31 | 61 | |
| Williams, Richard L. | N70 | 594 | |
| Williams, Robert Gale | | | |
| | N70 | 957 | |

| | | | |
|---|---|---|---|
| Williams, Roy Cox | N70 | 538 | |
| Williams, Thomas H. | M78 | 39 | |
| Williams, W. Tate | W49 | 420 | |
| Williams, Walter J. | N70 | 383 | |
| Williams, Warren W. | Dav | 1262 | |
| | Elk | 414 | |
| Williams, Warren Willard | | | |
| | Geo | 358 | |
| Williams, William H. | Dav | 1266 | |
| Williams, Winfield S. | | | |
| | Scr | 2:490 | |
| Williams, Yale | Lam | 311 | |
| Williams, Zeddie A. | N70 | 532 | |
| Williamson, Charles | Ang | 575 | |
| Williamson, David E.W. | | | |
| | Scr | 2:378 | |
| Williamson, David Edward | | | |
| Waite | W31 | 62 | |
| Williamson, George | Lam | 311 | |
| Willis, Nelson Winton | | | |
| | O'B | 130 | |
| Willis, Vernon Browning | | | |
| | W49 | 420 | |
| Willis, William | Lam | 311 | |
| Wilslef, Thomas | Dav | 1264 | |
| Wilson, A. | Lam | 311 | |
| Wilson, Ace | Gil | 3 | |
| Wilson, Alvira | Whi | 353 | |
| Wilson, B.F. | Ban | 269 | |
| Wilson, Benjamin B. | Scr | 3:289 | |
| Wilson, David | Wre | 557 | |
| Wilson, Dudley E. (Dud) | | | |
| | W49 | 420 | |
| Wilson, Embree Dewey | Ros | 97 | |
| Wilson, Frederick W. | W31 | 62 | |
| Wilson, G.W. | Moh | 43 | |
| Wilson, George F. | Scr | 3:420 | |
| Wilson, George W. | Scr | 3:352 | |
| | Wre | 557 | |
| Wilson, Hugh M. | Cur | 95 | |
| Wilson, Hugh Marion | Ros | 82 | |
| Wilson, Jack | Chr | 25 | |
| Wilson, Jim A.E. | Bix | 187 | |
| Wilson, Joseph I. | Scr | 2:503 | |
| Wilson, Loyd | L49 | Alpha | |
| L51 Alpha; | W49 | 23 | |
| Wilson, Luther | N24 | 294 | |
| Wilson, Maggie | Gil | 2 | |
| Wilson, Nathaniel E. | Scr | 3:93 | |
| Wilson, Nathaniel Estes | | | |
| | Wre | 566 | |
| Wilson, Orville R. | W49 | 421 | |
| Wilson, Paul K. | N24 | 295 | |
| Wilson, Thomas | W07 | 254 | |
| Wilson, Thomas Cave | W49 | 421 | |
| Wilson, Thomas R.C. | A82 | 125 | |
| A83 79; | A85 | 81 | |
| L73 xxiii; | L75 | xxxiii | |
| L77 xxxi; | L79 | xxxviii | |
| L81 xli; | L83 | xlvi | |
| | L85 | xlvi | |

# BIBLIOGRAPHY OF BOOKS INDEXED

(Listed in Alphabetical Order by Author or Title)


American Mothers Committee. MOTHERS OF ACHIEVEMENT IN AMERICAN HISTORY, 1776-1976: BI-CENTENNIAL PROJECT, 1974-1976. Rutland, Vt.: C.E. Tuttle Co., 1976. Symbol used in Index: Ame.

Angel, Myron, ed. HISTORY OF NEVADA; WITH ILLUSTRATIONS AND BIOGRAPHICAL SKETCHES OF ITS PROMINENT MEN AND PIONEERS. Oakland, Calif.: Thompson and West, 1881. Symbol used in Index: Ang.

Arrington, Leonard J. THE MORMONS IN NEVADA. Las Vegas, Nev.: Las Vegas Sun, 1979. Symbol used in Index: Arr.

Bancroft, Hubert Howe. HISTORY OF NEVADA, COLORADO, AND WYOMING, 1540-1888. The Works of Hubert Howe Bancroft, Volume XXV. San Francisco: The History Co., 1890. Symbol used in Index: Ban.

Binheim, Max, ed. WOMEN OF THE WEST; A SERIES OF BIOGRAPHICAL SKETCHES OF LIVING EMINENT WOMEN IN THE ELEVEN WESTERN STATES OF THE UNITED STATES OF AMERICA. 1928 Edition. Compiled and edited by Max Binheim, Editor-in-chief, Charles A. Elvin, Associate Editor. Los Angeles: Publishers Press, 1928. Symbol used in Index: Bin.

BIOGRAPHY OF DISTRICT COURT JUDGES, BEGINNING 1861. Reno: 196- Symbol used in Index: Jud.

Bixler, W.K. A DOZEN SIERRA SUCCESS STORIES; TWELVE INDIVIDUALISTS OF OUR TIME: EVA ADAMS, NORMAN BILTZ, PAUL CLAIBORNE, CLEL GEORGETTA, HARVEY GROSS, RAYMOND KNISLEY, WAYNE POULSEN, GEORGE PROBASCO, ARCHIE D. STEVENOT, LESTER D. SUMMERFIELD, HARVEY WEST, JIM A.E. WILSON. Tahoe Valley, Calif., 1964. Symbol used in Index: Bix.

Bruner, Firmin. SOME REMEMBERED...SOME FORGOT: LIFE IN CENTRAL NEVADA MINING CAMPS. Carson City: Nevada State Park Natural History Association, 1974. Symbol used in Index: Bru.

CHRONOLOGY AND DOCUMENTARY HANDBOOK OF THE STATE OF NEVADA. Chronologies and Documentary Handbooks of the States, v. 28. Dodds Ferry, N.Y.: Oceana Publications, 1978. Symbol used in Index: Chr.

Cronan, John. NEVADA MEN AND WOMEN OF ACHIEVEMENT.
Las Vegas: Privately Published, 1966. Symbol used in
Index: Cro.

Curran, Evalin, comp. HISTORY OF THE ORDER OF THE
EASTERN STAR, STATE OF NEVADA. s.l.: Order of the
Eastern Star, Grand Chapter of Nevada, 1949. Symbol
used in Index: Cur.

Davis, Samuel Post, ed. THE HISTORY OF NEVADA. 2
vols. Los Angeles: The Elms Publishing Co., 1913.
Symbol used in Index: Dav.

Dutton, Alfred H., and Lovey, Alan L. CARTOONS AND
CARICATURES OF MEN WHO MADE GOOD IN NEVADA. Salt Lake
City: A.H. Dutton and A.L. Lovey, 1907. Symbol used in
Index: D07.

Dutton, Alfred H. NOTABLE NEVADANS IN CARICATURE.
1915. Symbol used in Index: D15.

Eterovich, Adam S. YUGOSLAVS IN NEVADA, 1859-1900:
CROATIANS/DALMATIANS, MONTENEGRINS, HERCEGOVINIANS.
San Francisco: R and E Research Associates, 1973.
Symbol used in Index: Ete.

Gardner, Paul K. NEVADA STORIES: PERSHING COUNTY. The
Lovelock Review-Miner, 1931-1966. Symbol used in
Index: Per.

Georgetta, Clel. GOLDEN FLEECE IN NEVADA. Reno:
Venture Publishing Co., 1972. Symbol used in Index:
Geo.

Geuder, Patricia A. PIONEER WOMEN OF NEVADA. Carson
City: Alpha Chi State of the Delta Gamma Society,
International and the Nevada Division of the American
Association of University Women, 1976. Symbol used in
Index: Geu.

Giles, Ruth. RENO LINKAGE. Reno: Privately Published,
1977. Symbol used in Index: Gil.

Goodwin, Charles Carroll. AS I REMEMBER THEM. Salt
Lake City: Salt Lake Commercial Club, 1913. Symbol
used in Index: Goo.

Gorman, Thomas Kiely. SEVENTY-FIVE YEARS OF CATHOLIC
LIFE IN NEVADA: PUBLISHED TO COMMEMMORATE THE DIAMOND
JUBILEE OF THE FOUNDING OF THE CHURCH IN NEVADA, 1860-
1935. Reno: 1935. Symbol used in Index: Gor.

Hanson, Herschelle, and Hanson, Genevieve. THE UNSUNG
HEROES OF ESMERALDA. Angwin, Calif.: Johnson and
Hanson, Publishers, 1972. Symbol used in Index: Esm.

Hawes, D.C. NEVADA'S CAPITAL AND OFFICIALS. Carson City: D.C. Hawes (Daily Tribune Print), 1895. Symbol used in Index: Haw.

Herlan, Barbara. GENERAL HISTORY OF FORT CHURCHILL; NOTES ON STUDY OF FORT CHURCHILL WITH CORRECTIONS AND ADDITIONAL INFORMATION FROM FRED I. GREEN. 1 vol. Carson City: 1964. Symbol used in Index: Chu.

Knudtsen, Molly Flagg. HERE IS OUR VALLEY. Helen Marye Thomas Memorial Series No. 1. Reno: Agricultural Experiment Station, Max C. Fleischmann College of Agriculture, University of Nevada, 1975. Symbol used in Index: Gra.

Knudtsen, Molly Flagg. JOE DEAN AND OTHER PIONEERS. Reno: College of Agriculture, University of Nevada-Reno, 1985. Symbol used in Index: G85.

Lewis, Oscar, ed. THE LIFE AND TIMES OF THE VIRGINIA CITY TERRITORIAL ENTERPRISE: BEING REMINISCENCES OF FIVE DISTINGUISHED COMSTOCK JOURNALISTS. Ashland, Ore.: Lewis Osborne, 1971. 53 p. Symbol used in Index: Lew.

Midmore, Joe. FNB: First National Bank of Nevada. Sparks: Western Printing and Publishing Co., 1975. Symbol used in Index: Mid.

Mohan, Hugh J. PEN PICTURES OF THE STATE OFFICERS, LEGISLATORS, PUBLIC OFFICIALS AND NEWSPAPER MEN, AT THE CAPITOL DURING THE NINTH SESSION NEVADA LEGISLATURE. Virginia, Nev.: Daily Stage Steam Printing House, 1879. Symbol used in Index: Moh.

Moore, Boyd. MEET MR. BY MR. MOORE, IN TWO SKETCHES. Reno: n.p., 1932. Symbol used in Index: M32.

Moore, Boyd. NEVADANS AND NEVADA. San Francisco: Boyd Moore, 1950. Symbol used in Index: M50.

Moore, Boyd. PERSONS IN THE FOREGROUND. 2 vols. Reno: n.p., 1915, 1917. Symbol used in Index: M15.

Murbarger, Nell. SOVEREIGNS OF THE SAGE; TRUE STORIES OF PEOPLE AND PLACES IN THE GREAT SAGEBRUSH KINGDOM OF THE WESTERN UNITED STATES. Palm Desert, Calif.: Desert Magazine Press, 1958. Symbol used in Index: Mur.

Myles, Myrtle Tate. NEVADA'S GOVERNORS FROM TERRITORIAL DAYS TO THE PRESENT, 1861-1971. Sparks, Nev.: Western Printing and Publishing Co., 1972. Symbol used in Index: Myl.

Nevada. Adjutant-General's Office. NEVADA'S GOLDEN
STARS. A MEMORIAL VOLUME DESIGNED AS A GIFT FROM THE
STATE OF NEVADA TO THE RELATIVES OF THOSE NEVADA HEROES
WHO DIED IN THE WORLD WAR. Reno: Printed by A. Carlisle
& Co. of Nevada, 1924. Symbol used in Index: N24.

NEVADA LEGISLATIVE ALMANAC, 1982. Las Vegas, Nev.:
Ackerman-Rorex Corp., 1982. Symbol used in Index:
A82.

NEVADA LEGISLATIVE ALMANAC, 1983. Las Vegas, Nev.:
Ackerman Information Corp., 1983. Symbol used in
Index: A83.

NEVADA LEGISLATIVE ALMANAC, 1985. Las Vegas, Nev.:
Ackerman Information Corp., 1985. Symbol used in
Index: A85.

Nevada. Legislative Counsel Bureau. LEGISLATIVE
MANUAL: STATE OF NEVADA; FORTY-THIRD SESSION OF THE
NEVADA LEGISLATURE, 1947. Carson City: State Printing
Office, 1947. Symbol used in Index: L47.

Nevada. Legislative Counsel Bureau. LEGISLATIVE
MANUAL: STATE OF NEVADA; FORTY-FOURTH SESSION OF THE
NEVADA LEGISLATURE, 1949. Carson City: State Printing
Office, 1949. Symbol used in Index: L49.

Nevada. Legislative Counsel Bureau. LEGISLATIVE
MANUAL: STATE OF NEVADA; FORTY-FIFTH SESSION OF THE
NEVADA LEGISLATURE, 1951. Carson City: State Printing
Office, 1951. Symbol used in Index: L51.

Nevada. Legislative Counsel Bureau. LEGISLATIVE
MANUAL: STATE OF NEVADA; FORTY-SIXTH SESSION OF THE
NEVADA LEGISLATURE, 1953. Carson City: State Printing
Office, 1953. Symbol used in Index: L53.

Nevada. Legislative Counsel Bureau. LEGISLATIVE
MANUAL: STATE OF NEVADA; FORTY-SEVENTH SESSION OF THE
NEVADA LEGISLATURE, 1955. Carson City: State Printing
Office, 1955. Symbol used in Index: L55.

Nevada. Legislative Counsel Bureau. LEGISLATIVE
MANUAL: STATE OF NEVADA; FORTY-EIGHTH SESSION OF THE
NEVADA LEGISLATURE, 1957. Carson City: State Printing
Office, 1957. Symbol used in Index: L57.

Nevada. Legislative Counsel Bureau. LEGISLATIVE
MANUAL: STATE OF NEVADA; FORTY-NINTH SESSION OF THE
NEVADA LEGISLATURE, 1959. Carson City: State Printing
Office, 1959. Symbol used in Index: L59.

Nevada. Legislative Counsel Bureau. LEGISLATIVE
MANUAL: STATE OF NEVADA; FIFTIETH SESSION OF THE NEVADA
LEGISLATURE, 1960. Carson City: State Printing Office,
1960. Symbol used in Index: L60.

Nevada. Legislative Counsel Bureau. LEGISLATIVE
MANUAL: STATE OF NEVADA; FIFTY-FIRST SESSION OF THE
NEVADA LEGISLATURE, 1961. Carson City: State Printing
Office, 1961. Symbol used in Index: L61.

Nevada. Legislative Counsel Bureau. LEGISLATIVE
MANUAL: STATE OF NEVADA; FIFTY-SECOND SESSION OF THE
NEVADA LEGISLATURE, 1963. Carson City: State Printing
Office, 1963. Symbol used in Index: L63.

Nevada. Legislative Counsel Bureau. LEGISLATIVE
MANUAL: STATE OF NEVADA; FIFTY-SEVENTH SESSION OF THE
NEVADA LEGISLATURE, 1973. Bulletin no. 103. Carson
City: State Printing Office, 1973. Symbol used in
Index: L73.

Nevada. Legislative Counsel Bureau. LEGISLATIVE
MANUAL: STATE OF NEVADA; FIFTY-EIGHTH SESSION OF THE
NEVADA LEGISLATURE, 1975. Bulletin no. 126. Carson
City: State Printing Office, 1975. Symbol used in
Index: L75.

Nevada. Legislative Counsel Bureau. LEGISLATIVE
MANUAL: STATE OF NEVADA; FIFTY-NINTH SESSION OF THE
NEVADA LEGISLATURE, 1977. Bulletin no. 77-23. Carson
City: State Printing Office, n.d. Symbol used in
Index: L77.

Nevada. Legislative Counsel Bureau. LEGISLATIVE
MANUAL: STATE OF NEVADA; SIXTIETH SESSION OF THE NEVADA
LEGISLATURE, 1979. Bulletin no. 79-21. Carson City:
State Printing Office, 1979. Symbol used in Index:
L79.

Nevada. Legislative Counsel Bureau. LEGISLATIVE
MANUAL: STATE OF NEVADA; SIXTY-FIRST SESSION OF THE
NEVADA LEGISLATURE, 1981. Bulletin no. 81-26. Carson
City: State Printing Office, 1981. Symbol used in
Index: L81.

Nevada. Legislative Counsel Bureau. LEGISLATIVE
MANUAL: STATE OF NEVADA; SIXTY-SECOND SESSION OF THE
NEVADA LEGISLATURE, 1983. Bulletin no. 83-13. Carson
City: State Printing Office, 1982. Symbol used in
Index: L82.

Nevada. Legislative Counsel Bureau. LEGISLATIVE
MANUAL: STATE OF NEVADA; SIXTY-THIRD SESSION OF THE
NEVADA LEGISLATURE, 1985. Bulletin no. 85-12. Carson
City: State Printing Office, 1985. Symbol used in
Index: L85.

Nevada State Historical Society. FIRST BIENNIAL REPORT
OF THE NEVADA HISTORICAL SOCIETY, 1907-1908. Carson
City: State Printing Office, 1909. Symbol used in
Index: N07.

Nevada State Historical Society. SECOND BIENNIAL
REPORT OF THE NEVADA HISTORICAL SOCIETY, 1909-1910.
Carson City: State Printing Office, 1911. Symbol used
in Index: N09.

Nevada State Historical Society. THIRD BIENNIAL REPORT
OF THE NEVADA HISTORICAL SOCIETY, 1911-1912. Carson
City: State Printing Office, 1913. Symbol used in
Index: N11.

THE NEVADA STATE LABOR TEMPLE REVIEW: OFFICIAL BUYING
GUIDE OF ORGANIZED LABOR FOR 1914-1915. Symbol used in
Index: Lab.

Nevada. State Library, Carson City. Reader's Service
Division. BRIEF BIOGRAPHICAL INFORMATION ON NEVADA
GOVERNORS. Carson City: Nevada State Library, 1959.
Symbol used in Index: N59.

NEVADA, THE SILVER STATE. 2 vols. Carson City:
Western States Historical Publishers, 1970. Symbol
used in Index: N70.

NOTABLE NEVADANS: SNAP-SHOTS OF SAGEBRUSHERS WHO ARE
DOING THINGS. Reno: n.p., 1910. Symbol used in Index:
N10.

O'Brien, John P., ed. HISTORY OF THE BENCH AND BAR OF
NEVADA. San Francisco: Bench and Bar Publishing Co.,
1913. Symbol used in Index: O'B.

PACIFIC COAST ANNUAL MINING REVIEW AND STOCK LEDGER,
1878-1879: CONTAINING DETAILED OFFICIAL REPORTS OF THE
PRINCIPAL GOLD AND SILVER MINES OF NEVADA, CALIFORNIA,
ARIZONA, UTAH, NEW MEXICO, AND IDAHO; A HISTORY AND
DESCRIPTION OF MINING AND STOCK DEALING ON THIS COAST
WITH BIOGRAPHICAL SKETCHES OF 100 OF THE PRINCIPAL MEN
ENGAGED THEREIN; AND A SERIES OF FINANCE ARTICLES BY
HENRY S. FITCH. San Francisco: Francis & Valentine,
1878. Symbol used in Index: M78.

PACIFIC COAST ANNUAL MINING REVIEW AND STOCK LEDGER,
1888. San Francisco: Francis & Valentine; San Francisco
Journal of Commerce, 1888. Symbol used in Index: M88.

Panaca Centennial Book Committee. A CENTURY IN MEADOW VALLEY, 1864-1964. Compiled and Edited by Panaca Centennial Book Committee, Ruth Lee and Sylvia Wadsworth, Co-chairmen. Panaca, Nev.: 1966. Symbol used in Index: Mea.

Patterson, Edna B. HALLECK COUNTRY, NEVADA: THE STORY OF THE LAND AND ITS PEOPLE. Reno: University of Nevada, Reno Press, 1982. Symbol used in Index: Hal.

Patterson, Edna B. SAGEBRUSH DOCTORS. Springville, Utah: Printed by Art City Publishing Co., 1972. Symbol used in Index: Doc.

Patterson, Edna B. THIS LAND WAS OURS; AN IN-DEPTH STUDY OF A FRONTIER COMMUNITY. Springville, Utah: Printed by Art City Publishing Co., 1973. Symbol used in Index: Lam.

Patterson, Edna B.; Ulph, Louise A.; and Goodwin, Victor. NEVADA'S NORTHEAST FRONTIER. Sparks, Nev.: Western Printing & Publishing Co., 1969. Symbol used in Index: Elk.

Phi Delta Kappa. WHO'S WHO IN NORTHERN NEVADA EDUCATION. A Bicentennial Project of Phi Delta Kappa '76, Featuring Brief Biographies and Photographs of Leaders in Education. Edward H. Howard and E.E. Loveless, Editors. Reno: Phi Delta Kappa, 1976. Symbol used in Index: Phi.

Powell, John J. NEVADA: THE LAND OF SILVER. San Francisco: Bacon, 1876. Symbol used in Index: Pow.

Ratay, Myra Sauer. PIONEERS OF THE PONDEROSA: HOW WASHOE VALLEY RESCUED THE COMSTOCK. Sparks, Nev.: Printed by Western Printing and Publishing Co., 1973. Symbol used in Index: Was.

Reifschneider, Olga. BIOGRAPHIES OF NEVADA BOTANISTS: 1844-1963. Reno: University of Nevada Press, 1964. Symbol used in Index: Rei.

Ross, Silas Earl. BIOGRAPHICAL SKETCHES OF NEVADA GRAND MASTERS, F.& A.M.; 1865-1970. Reno: 1970. Symbol used in Index: Ros.

Scrugham, James Graves, ed. NEVADA; A NARRATIVE OF THE CONQUEST OF A FRONTIER LAND; COMPRISING THE STORY OF HER PEOPLE FROM THE DAWN OF HISTORY TO THE PRESENT TIME. 3 vols. New York: The American Historical Society, 1935. Symbol used in Index: Scr.

Shuck, Oscar Tully, ed. REPRESENTATIVE AND LEADING MEN
OF THE PACIFIC: BEING ORIGINAL SKETCHES OF THE LIVES
AND CHARACTERS OF THE PRINCIPAL MEN, TO WHICH ARE ADDED
THEIR SPEECHES, ADDRESSES, ORATIONS, EULOGIES, LECTURES
AND POEMS, INCLUDING THE HAPPIEST FORENSIC EFFORTS OF
BAKER, RANDOLPH, MCDOUGALL, T. STARR KING, AND OTHER
POPULAR ORATORS. San Francisco: Bacon and Co., 1870.
Symbol used in Index: Shu.

Silen, Sol. LA HISTORIA DE LOS VASCONGADOS EN EL OESTE
DE LOS ESTADOS UNIDOS. Traducciones por Manuel J. de
Galvan. New York: Las Novedades, 1917. Boise:
Mountain States Publishers, 1918. Symbol used in
Index: Sil.

SKETCHES OF THE INTER-MOUNTAIN STATES: TOGETHER WITH
BIOGRAPHIES OF MANY PROMINENT AND PROGRESSIVE CITIZENS
WHO HAVE HELPED IN THE DEVELOPMENT AND HISTORY-MAKING
OF THIS MARVELOUS REGION: 1847-1909: UTAH, IDAHO,
NEVADA. Salt Lake City, Utah: Salt Lake Tribune, 1909.
Symbol used in Index: Ske.

The Successful American. PORTRAITS AND BIOGRAPHIES OF
PROMINENT ENGINEERS, MINERS AND BUSINESS MEN OF
NEVADA.... New York: Writers' Press Association, 1906.
Symbol used in Index: Suc.

Taylor, Maude Sawin. FROM MY NEVADA NOTEBOOK. Sparks,
Nev.: Western Printing and Publishing Co., 1965.
Symbol used in Index: Tay.

Walton, Clifford C. NEVADA TODAY: A PICTORIAL VOLUME
OF THE STATE'S ACTIVITIES. Portland, Oreg.: Capitol
Publishing Co., 1949. Symbol used in Index: W49.

WHITE RIVER VALLEY THEN AND NOW, 1898-1980. Provo,
Utah: Melayne Printing, 1981. Symbol used in Index:
Whi.

WHO'S WHO IN NEVADA: BIOGRAPHICAL DICTIONARY OF MEN AND
WOMEN WHO ARE BUILDING A STATE. Vol. 1, 1931-32.
Reno: Who's Who in Nevada Publishing Co., 1932. Symbol
used in Index: W31.

WHO'S WHO IN NEVADA: BRIEF SKETCHES OF MEN WHO ARE
MAKING HISTORY IN THE SAGEBRUSH STATE. Published by
Bessie Beatty. Los Angeles: Home Printing Co., 1907.
Symbol used in Index: W07.

Wren, Thomas. A HISTORY OF THE STATE OF NEVADA: ITS
RESOURCES AND PEOPLE. New York: The Lewis Publishing
Co., 1904. Symbol used in Index: Wre.

BIBLIOGRAPHIES USED FOR SELECTION OF BOOKS INDEXED

California. State Library, Sacramento. Sutro Branch,
San Francisco. LOCAL HISTORY CATALOG. 29 microfiche.
Bellevue, Wash.: Commercial Microfilm Service, under
contract to the California State Library, 1982.


Elwell, Margaret, comp. A BIBLIOGRAPHY OF HUMBOLDT
COUNTY. Winnemucca, Nev.: Humboldt County Library,
1985.


Filby, P. William, comp. A BIBLIOGRAPHY OF AMERICAN
COUNTY HISTORIES. Baltimore: Genealogical Publishing
Co., 1985.


Genealogical Department. GENEALOGICAL LIBRARY CATALOG.
Salt Lake City: Genealogical Department, 1985.


Paher, Stanley W. NEVADA: AN ANNOTATED BIBLIOGRAPHY:
BOOKS & PAMPHLETS RELATING TO THE HISTORY & DEVELOPMENT
OF THE SILVER STATE. Las Vegas: Nevada Publications,
1980.


U.S. Library of Congress. UNITED STATES LOCAL
HISTORIES IN THE LIBRARY OF CONGRESS: A BIBLIOGRAPHY.
5 vols. Baltimore: Magna Carta Book Co., 1975.

# BIBLIOGRAPHY OF STATEWIDE BIOGRAPHICAL INDEXES

## California

Parker, J. Carlyle. AN INDEX TO THE BIOGRAPHEES IN 19TH CENTURY CALIFORNIA COUNTY HISTORIES. Gale Genealogy and Local History Series, vol. 7. Detroit: Gale Research Co., 1979. OCLC 4832150. LCCN 79-11900. 979.4/04/0922. Z5313.U6C36 F860.
>    Contains approximately 16,500 entries for sixty-one county histories.

## Colorado

Bromwell, Henriette Elizabeth. COLORADO PORTRAIT AND BIOGRAPHY INDEX. 5 vols. on 2 reels of microfilm. Denver: n.p. 1935. OCLC 4044268. F775.B76.
>    This index is available for purchase from the Denver Public Library, 1357 Broadway, Denver, CO 80203.

## Georgia

THE LIBRARY OF CONGRESS INDEX TO BIOGRAPHIES IN STATE AND LOCAL HISTORIES. Microfilm. 40 reels. Baltimore: Magna Carta Book Co., 1979.
>    This index is a national index and contains approximately 170,000 entries to biographees in 340 titles in the Library of Congress. Georgia has the second largest number of titles indexed with 36. Other states included in the index that are not included in this list are Alabama with 8 titles indexed; Arizona, 6; Arkansas, 10; Idaho, 12; Mississippi, 13; North Carolina, 10; South Carolina, 13; and the other thirty-six states with 3 or less.

## Illinois

ILLINOIS BIOGRAPHICAL INDEX. West Bountiful, Utah: Genealogical Indexing Associates, forthcoming. Microfiche.
>    This index already contains over 100,000 names and will contain nearly 300,000 names. For a small fee it may be consulted before publication by mail. Address inquiries to the publisher, P.O. Box 102, West Bountiful, UT 84087. The titles held by the Illinois State Library, Springfield are identified.

Indiana

INDIANA BIOGRAPHICAL INDEX.  West Bountiful, Utah:
Genealogical Indexing Associates, 1983.  16 microfiche.
Contains 247,423 name entries to 537 state,
county, city, and local histories.  Many of the
books indexed are identified as being available at
the Indiana State Library in Indianapolis.  Titles
available at the Genealogical Department Library
in Salt Lake City and the Brigham Young
University, Harold B. Lee Library in Provo, Utah
are also identified.


Iowa

Morford, Charles.  BIOGRAPHICAL INDEX TO THE COUNTY
HISTORIES OF IOWA.  Baltimore: Gateway Press, 1979.
OCLC 5336698.  LCCN 79-87902.  977.7/00992.  Z1283.M66
F620 (May be purchased from the author, Lanyon, Iowa
50544).
Contains 40,540 entries of the biographees in
131 of the 251 county histories for all of Iowa's
ninety-nine counties.


Kentucky

THE LIBRARY OF CONGRESS INDEX TO BIOGRAPHIES IN STATE
AND LOCAL HISTORIES.  Microfilm.  40 reels.  Baltimore:
Magna Carta Book Co., 1979.
This index is explained in the above entry
for Georgia.  Kentucky has the largest number of
titles indexed with 50.


Louisiana

THE LIBRARY OF CONGRESS INDEX TO BIOGRAPHIES IN STATE
AND LOCAL HISTORIES.  Microfilm.  40 reels.  Baltimore:
Magna Carta Book Co., 1979.
Contains 21 titles for Louisiana.  See the
Georgia entry, above, for more information about
the collection.


Maryland

Passano, Eleanor Phillips.  AN INDEX OF THE SOURCE
RECORDS OF MARYLAND: GENEALOGICAL, BIOGRAPHICAL,
HISTORICAL.  Baltimore, 1940.  Reprint.  Baltimore:
Genealogical Publishing Co., 1974.
Contains over 27,000 entries to seventy titles.

Michigan

Loomis, Frances, comp. MICHIGAN BIOGRAPHY INDEX.
Detroit: Detroit Public Library, 1946. 4 reels of
microfilm. Woodbridge, Conn.: Research Publications,
1973. OCLC 3646166.
     Contains approximately 73,000 names of the
biographees in 361 biographical directories, city
and county directories and histories.
Availability of nearly all titles is identified
for thirty-five Michigan libraries.


Nevada

Parker, J. Carlyle, and Parker, Janet G. NEVADA
BIOGRAPHICAL AND GENEALOGICAL SKETCH INDEX. Turlock,
Calif.: Marietta Pubishing Co., 1986.
     Contains 7,230 biographees in biographical
and genealogical sketches in eight-six state,
regional, county, and city histories and
biographical directories of Nevada published
between 1870 and 1985.


New York

"The New York State Biographical, Genealogical and
Portrait Index." Personal index of Gunther E. Pohl, 24
Walden Place, Great Neck, N.Y. 11020.
     This index contains entries to the
biographical sketches and portraits in about nine
hundred New York state, county, city, and
community histories. Mr. Pohl will consult this
index for patrons and provide them with
bibliographic citations and page numbers for a
moderate fee. All correspondence to him must
include a self-addressed stamped envelope.


Ohio

Ohio Historical Society. OHIO COUNTY HISTORY SURNAME
INDEX. 64 reels of microfilm. Columbus, Ohio: 1984.
     Contains over 450,000 names. Reels may be
purchased or borrowed on interlibary loan for a
prepaid fee.

## Oregon

Brandt, Patricia, and Guilford, Nancy, eds. OREGON
BIOGRAPHY INDEX. Oregon State University Bibliographic
Series, no. 11. Corvallis: Oregon State University,
1976. OCLC 2388703 LCCN 76-366322. 920/.0795.
Z5305.U5B7. CT256.
     Contains over 18,000 names to biographees
     from forty-six histories.


## Tennessee

THE LIBRARY OF CONGRESS INDEX TO BIOGRAPHIES IN STATE
AND LOCAL HISTORIES. Microfilm. 40 reels. Baltimore:
Magna Carta Book Co., 1979.
     Tennessee has the third largest number of
     titles indexed in this collection with 32. See
     the Georgia entry above for details about other
     states in the collection.


## Texas

THE LIBRARY OF CONGRESS INDEX TO BIOGRAPHIES IN STATE
AND LOCAL HISTORIES. Microfilm. 40 reels. Baltimore:
Magna Carta Book Co., 1979.
     Texas has 27 titles indexed in the
     collection. The above entry for Georgia contains
     more details about this collection.


## Utah

Wiggins, Marvin E., comp. MORMONS AND THEIR NEIGHBORS:
AN INDEX TO OVER 75,000 BIOGRAPHICAL SKETCHES FROM 1820
TO THE PRESENT. 2 vols. Provo, Utah: Harold B. Lee
Library, Brigham Young University, 1984. OCLC:
     Indexes 194 titles.

OTHER BOOKS BY J. CARLYLE PARKER


PENNSYLVANIA AND MIDDLE ATLANTIC STATES GENEALOGICAL
MANUSCRIPTS: A USER'S GUIDE TO THE MANUSCRIPT
COLLECTIONS OF THE GENEALOGICAL SOCIETY OF PENNSYLVANIA
AS INDEXED IN ITS MANUSCRIPT MATERIALS INDEX;
MICROFILMED BY THE GENEALOGICAL DEPARTMENT, SALT LAKE
CITY. Turlock, Calif.: Marietta Publishing Co, 1986.


DIRECTORY OF ARCHIVIST AND LIBRARIAN GENEALOGICAL
INSTRUCTORS. Turlock, Calif.: Marietta Publishing Co.,
1985.


LIBRARY SERVICE FOR GENEALOGISTS. Gale Genealogy and
Local History Series, v. 15. Detroit: Gale Research
Co., 1981.


AN INDEX TO THE BIOGRAPHEES IN 19TH CENTURY CALIFORNIA
COUNTY HISTORIES. Gale Genealogy and Local History
Series, v. 7. Detroit: Gale Research Co., 1979.


CITY, COUNTY, TOWN, AND TOWNSHIP INDEX TO THE 1850
FEDERAL CENSUS SCHEDULES. Gale Genealogy and Local
History Series, v. 6. Detroit: Gale Research Co.,
1979.


A PERSONAL NAME INDEX TO RECORDS OF CALIFORNIA MEN IN
THE WAR OF THE REBELLION, 1861 TO 1867, COMPILED BY
BRIG.-GEN. RICHARD H. ORTON... Gale Genealogy and
Local History Series, v. 5. Detroit: Gale Research
Co., 1978.

# ABOUT THE AUTHORS

Janet G. Parker, a former school teacher, started
genealogical research as a teenager and has taken
several genealogical courses at Brigham Young
University. She has taught genealogical classes for
the LDS Church and has been a research seminar
instructor. Since 1978 she has been a volunteer
library assistant at the Modesto Branch Genealogical
Library.

During the summer of 1983 she assisted Mr. Parker
in presenting sixteen day-long genealogical mini-
courses for genealogists and librarians in eight cities
from Denver, Colorado to Worcester, Massachusetts.
From 1982 to 1985 she also aided him in a highly
successful university course and research trips to the
Genealogical Society Library in Salt Lake City and to
research centers in Washington, D.C.

J. Carlyle Parker is Head of Public Services and
Assistant Library Director, California State
University, Stanislaus, and has taught historical and
genealogical research courses for the University. In
1968 as a volunteer he organized and continues to
direct the Modesto Branch Genealogical Library of the
Church of Jesus Christ of Latter-day Saints.

He has written numerous genealogical articles and
book reviews, compiled indexes and union lists, edited
the fifteen volume Gale Genealogy and Local History
Series, and is author of four books in the series
including the series' second best seller, LIBRARY
SERVICE FOR GENEALOGISTS. In 1984 the National
Genealogical Society presented him with an Award of
Merit and the Utah Genealogical Association selected
him as a Fellow of the Association.

He has taught at numerous genealogical seminars
and workshops for genealogists and/or librarians in
British Columbia, California, Colorado, Iowa,
Massachusetts, Missouri, Nebraska, Nevada, New York,
Ohio, Oregon, Pennsylvania, Utah, and Washington, D.C.
He presented papers at both World Conference on Records
in Salt Lake City, has taught at six of the
genealogical seminars at Brigham Young University, and
also at the National Institute on Genealogical Research
at the National Archives in Washington, D.C. in 1979.